To Kathy,   July 2018

Best wishes for Your Health
                    &
           Balance!

                              Joe Marson

SQUARE
one
A SIMPLE GUIDE TO A
BALANCED LIFE

PATRICK MULCAHY, *Chairman of the Board of Energizer Holdings*
"I can heartily recommend *Square One* to any reader, young or old. While it's the story of Dr. Joe's journey to rebalance his life, it provides all of us with a way to visualize where we are...and if we find ourselves out of balance, it offers the necessary steps to get us back to square one."

DR. ROBIN WEST, *Medical Director of Inova Sports Medicine and Director of Sports Medicine for the Washington Redskins*
"Following William Danforth's concept of 'living tools,' Dr. Maroon eloquently describes how squaring up his life helped him rise up from his lowest point and get back on a path to complete fulfillment of his body, mind, heart, and soul."

DR. W. LEE WARREN, *author of* No Place to Hide: A Surgeon's Long Journey Home from the Iraq War
"I wanted to be a brain surgeon, but I quickly felt unsure of my place in a profession where the doctors' resolve to succeed was often as cold and sharp as the steel from which their scalpels were formed. Dr. Maroon took me aside and said, 'You can spend your life trying to be the best, but you'll never be *your* best unless you learn balance.' In *Square One*, readers follow Dr. Maroon from the pit to the summit of a remarkable life and right back to square one. Thank you, Joe. We all need this book."

MARK I. GREENE, *partner at Cravath, Swaine & Moore and leader of its international practice*
"I cannot thank Dr. Maroon enough for writing this fascinating and inspiring life story. I honestly didn't want *Square One* to end because each page resonated so deeply. Countless readers will benefit from its simple yet often-overlooked truths about what it takes to live a balanced, rich, and fulfilling life."

Square One: A Simple Guide to a Balanced Life
Joseph Maroon MD with Carrie Kennedy MEd
Includes index
ISBN 978-0-9983509-0-5
Library of Congress Control Number: 2016961094

For Laura, Jonathan, Lisa,
Adara, Isabella, and Emma,
and in loving memory of Michael

SQUARE
One

A SIMPLE GUIDE TO A
BALANCED LIFE

TABLE OF CONTENTS

10

I MET DR. JOE MAROON MANY YEARS AGO when he joined me as a board member of the American Youth Foundation (AYF). It was clear that Dr. Joe and I were of like minds, perhaps because of our modest Catholic upbringing. Yet Joe had such a quiet grace that it was some time before I learned he was a renowned neurosurgeon, a Pittsburgh Steelers physician, a triathlete…and now the author of this important work. After reading Joe's manuscript, I've also come to understand that like Joe, my exposure to the AYF and its teaching changed my life for the better.

As a senior at Cornell University, I was awarded a Danforth Fellowship from the foundation set up by William H. Danforth. In addition to a cash stipend, there was a two-week summer component for the 50 fellowship winners, one chosen from each state's land grant college. We gathered first in St. Louis—the location of the headquarters of Danforth's Ralston Purina Company—and met with leaders in the fields of business, medicine, and education. The second week of the symposium, we "Danny Boys" were trooped up to the AYF's Camp Miniwanca in Michigan, where we were exposed to the AYF's mantra: "My own self, at my very best, all the time." It was here that I first saw Danforth's concept of "four-square living" in action, learning about the importance of the four key components of our lives: our physical health, our spirituality, our mental capabilities, and our relationships.

During this week, we spent quality time with several guests, including an Anglican bishop, a senator, a university president, and the CEO of a major company. This was a heady experience for a young man. In conversations with these leaders, however, I realized they were just people like me, but they'd found something they loved to do and worked hard to do it. That Aha! moment changed my life, and I am forever grateful for the teachings of the AYF and its founder, William H. Danforth.

After graduate school, the Ralston Purina Company offered me a summer internship, and I took the job simply because I liked the people. After a two-year stint in the United States army, I returned in 1969 and started my career as a marketing assistant. Twenty-eight years later, having continued to work with great people on challenging assignments, I was named co-CEO of the company. In 2000, we spun out Energizer Holdings as a NYSE company, and I took the CEO position.

If you'd asked me to draw my "square" during the earlier years of my career, it would've looked like a two-by-four: long on the mental and physical sides, shorter on the relationship and spiritual ones. I was certainly not "my own self, at my very best, all the time." Then dark days came when my wife of nearly 30 years, with whom I share four children, initiated a divorce. So I embarked on a period of self-awareness, doing several of the exercises outlined in Danforth's book *I Dare You*. I took the short course on one of his exercises, so rather than writing out a whole eulogy for myself, I considered my epitaph. After a lot of soul searching, I believe that what Danforth called Spirit led me to this statement: "He was loved by his children." This became a comforting thought to help me regain my footing.

At this stage of my life, my square isn't perfect either, but it's because I'm very long on "relationships" and have brought more play into my life. I'm happy and content with exactly where I am and see now that, over the long haul, it all seems to have balanced out.

I can heartily recommend *Square One* to any reader, young or old. And one doesn't need to be in crisis to get a great deal out of this book. While it's the story of Dr. Joe's journey to rebalance his life, it provides all of us with a way to visualize where we are…and if we find ourselves out of balance, it offers the necessary steps to get us back to square one.

Thanks go out to you, Joe, for sharing this work with us.

Pat Mulcahy
Chairman of the Board, Energizer Holdings

Four Square

You have not one, but four lives to live—
a four-fold opportunity to grow. A body, a brain, a heart, and a soul—
these are our living tools.
To use them is not a task. It is a golden opportunity.

— William H. Danforth, *I Dare You*

SINCE ANCIENT TIMES, the number four has represented order, stability, solidarity, and support. We see four points on a compass; we mark the passage of four seasons; we recognize the four elements of fire, wind, water, and air.

The number four is also embodied in the straight and regular sides of a square, a geometric shape easily recognized by the average toddler. The square is so common, in fact, and so decidedly lacking in interesting angles that it's developed a reputation for being just a little boring. The twentieth century saw the rise of the term "square" to refer to a person who was old-fashioned or out of touch, and when we're encouraged to think creatively, we're told we must think "outside of the box."

So can I make the case that this humble little shape had a profound impact on my life? Can I get you to see that "in the box" thinking can significantly improve the quality of your experiences? Can I prove that it's actually cool to be square? The point of this book is to show how a life radically out of balance can be reshaped using the simple concept of a square, which leads to better health, a deeper sense of awe, more meaningful work, and more joyful relationships. Simply put, it's time to square up your life.

By the age of 41, I'd achieved a great deal of professional success, but my life was dangerously—nearly fatally—out of balance. Unfortunately, I was also completely unaware of what a wreck my life had become. What allowed me to find my footing was a little leather-bound book, William Danforth's *I Dare You*, which I'd received as a prize at my high school graduation nearly 25 years earlier. This slim volume laid out the clear and basic philosophy that our lives are essentially composed of four elements: our health, our spirituality, our work, and our relationships. Danforth's direct language and simple metaphor of a square gave me profound insight into what—in retrospect—was obvious burnout, including emotional and physical exhaustion, increased cynicism, and a loss of purpose and compassion. Danforth's way of thinking finally gave me the tools to help me get healthier, identify priorities, make conscious choices, and begin to build a more balanced life.

Several years later, I was invited to deliver a lecture to over 2,000 neurosurgeons and addressed the topic of physician burnout and the concept of work/life balance. I introduced Danforth's square and spoke about how one-dimensional, work-focused living can result in compromised patient care, damaged social relationships, and the atrophy of both the physical and spiritual sides of life. This presentation had the biggest impact of any I'd ever given, and I've had nothing but positive reactions from other lectures on the square; audience members have said the philosophy encouraged them to find more fulfillment at work, rejuvenate their relationships, improve their health and energy, and embrace a new sense of self.

Now with increasing science to support the need to "square up" our lives, I want to share my experiences to encourage you to find the benefits and beauty of a life truly in balance. Recent Nobel Prize–winning discoveries in both traditional and emerging fields of neuroscience have converged to explain the intricate mind-body connections related to healthy, purposeful living. While we once thought brain cells were finite, for instance, we now know brains actually produce new cells and that this birth of new neurons—called neurogenesis—is prompted primarily by physical activity and stress reduction. We also understand the brain's remarkable neuroplasticity, which is its potential to create new neural pathways and adapt to new situations.

The new science of epigenetics (literally, "above genetics") has also radically changed the long-held belief that our genes somehow spell out our destiny. By mapping the human genome, we know that what we eat, how we exercise and manage stress, our lifestyle choices, and the very thoughts we think activate powerful changes at the most basic genetic levels. We can actually turn up to 70 percent of our genes "on" or "off"—for better or for worse—through our choices and habits. Such revolutionary new discoveries give us an amazing opportunity to rethink our approach to living: we actually have much more control over our health and the essential quality of our lives than we ever believed possible.

The goal of this book is to keep the medical information understandable and applicable, and to mix it in with anecdotes from my own life and from others who are doing remarkable things on their own powerful, fulfilling journeys. You'll learn about athlete Rajesh Durbal—the first triple amputee to complete an Ironman triathlon—and how he empowers people around the world to seek their purpose and celebrate the amazing potential of the human spirit. You'll see how the dynamic neurosurgeon Dr. Elizabeth Tyler-Kabara balances her family life with her revolutionary work with paralyzed patients and thought-controlled robotics. And you'll appreciate poet Sam Hazo's story of how strong relationships have allowed him to thrive both personally and professionally over the course of his long life.

A book about finding balance wouldn't be complete without a look into three topics fundamental to experiencing true fulfillment: humor, creativity, and the uniquely powerful feeling that Mihaly Csikszentmihalyi calls "flow." So chapter 9 celebrates these topics and discusses how to seek them out in all areas of our lives. And finally, to relay how the concept of square living can help children develop lifelong health and balance, Anna Kay Vorsteg will offer insights from her perspective as the president of the American Youth Foundation, an organization based on William H. Danforth's powerful philosophies.

We all possess a body, a brain, a heart, and a soul, which means we have an incredible opportunity and an incredible responsibility to put these "living tools" to work. Just as William Danforth dared me to be a better person with his bold little book, I now dare *you* to find a healthier, more fulfilling, more balanced life. ◻

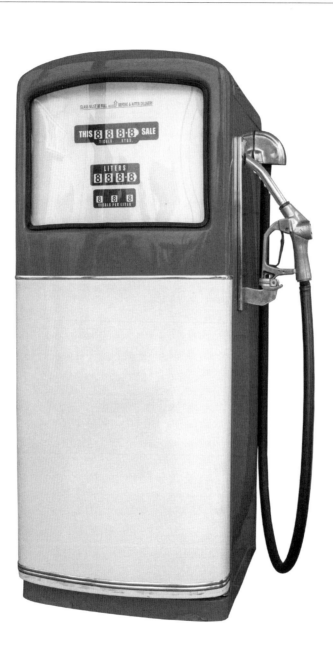

Running on Empty

*The life of every man is a diary in which he means to write
one story, and writes another; and his humblest hour is when he
compares the volume as it is with what he vowed to make it.*

— James Matthew Barrie

FLIPPING HAMBURGERS and working at gas stations are jobs some people might do during the summer months in high school, or maybe to make a living if they haven't pursued a higher education. I, however, did both of these jobs at the age of 41, after I'd been a successful neurosurgeon for over a decade. Decidedly out of order on a résumé, right? But exactly one week after serving as the chief neurosurgeon in an operating room at a premier teaching hospital in Pittsburgh, I was filling up 18-wheelers and figuring out how to use the deep fryer at a truck stop in the small town of Wheeling, located in West Virginia's northern panhandle.

The implausibility of all of this may sound like the premise for a 1970s sitcom, with funny character actors playing the truckers who frequented the joint. But I can attest that this was all quite real and—unfortunately for me—not funny at all. Only in retrospect can I see that the reason behind this unlikely turn of events was quite simple: my life was completely out of balance. After years of study and sacrifice, I'd thrown everything I had into my career as a surgeon—writing scientific papers, earning academic titles, and gaining peer approval and international recognition. Yet I'd pushed every other part of my life—my relationship with my parents and siblings, my marriage, my vital role as a father, my own health, my spiritual beliefs—out of the way to pursue the amulets of success. And when everything came crashing down, I finally understood author James Barrie's metaphor that opened this chapter: the story I'd written was nothing like what I'd vowed to write.

IT WAS EARLY JANUARY, 1979, and I was chief of neurosurgery at Presbyterian University Hospital in Pittsburgh. After a grueling eight-hour operation to try and save a patient's life, the pathologist determined the brain tumor we'd battled was malignant, and the patient had little chance of survival. When I'd driven to the hospital early that morning, a light snow had been falling, but by the time I drove home at the end of the day, I was in the midst of a ferocious winter storm.

Already feeling miserable and exhausted, I unlocked the front door to my house and was paralyzed by the sight of empty rooms. I had known my 15-year marriage was struggling, but my wife had obviously reached the breaking point. She'd taken everything except my clothes, a bed, and some lawn furniture now set up in the living room and had driven away in a rented U-Haul in the blinding snow. She'd also taken our two children—a son who was ten, and a daughter nearly five—and moved to Chicago to be closer to family and friends, seeking the support she so desperately needed. I was devastated.

....

After years of study and sacrifice, I'd thrown everything I had into my career as a surgeon—writing scientific papers, earning academic titles, and gaining peer approval and international recognition. Yet I'd pushed every other part of my life—my relationship with my parents and siblings, my marriage, my vital role as a father, my own health, my spiritual beliefs— out of the way to pursue the amulets of success.

The surgeries I performed over the next few weeks, even the uncomplicated ones, were difficult. But when one of my patients began hemorrhaging on the operating table, I was hit with an anxiety I'd never known. Like a scuba diver cut off from his oxygen supply, I panicked and had to ask a colleague for help. We completed the surgery successfully, but afterwards, I could barely stand up.

In the corner of a vacant operating room, I slid to the floor and cried, struck by what I can only describe as a wave of emptiness and fear. My wife and children were gone, and I was mentally depleted and in horrible health. I'd also lost all connection to my faith, which had helped me gain perspective during other difficult times in my life. I didn't want to stay at the hospital a second longer, but I dreaded going out in the cold and facing my depressingly barren house.

Then it got worse.

After returning home, a phone call jarred me from my sleep at two o'clock in the morning: the police had found my 60-year-old father dead in his office. We would later learn it was a massive heart attack—a complete blockage of his anterior descending artery known as the "widow maker's artery"—but while I was racing to get to my mother in Bridgeport, Ohio, my mind was going through every possible cause for my father's death. I was overwhelmed and within days would resign from my job as chief of neurosurgery with the concern that I might never be able to practice again. I would not return to Pittsburgh for over a year.

IT WAS A BITTERLY COLD January in the Ohio Valley, and the air was frigid during my father's funeral. The next day, I drove the few miles from Bridgeport, over the frozen Ohio River and into Wheeling, West Virginia. My purpose? I had to take stock of the dilapidated and debt-ridden truck stop my father had bequeathed to my mother and me. As I pulled into the parking lot, I looked directly across Interstate 70 at our competition, a sprawling modern hub called Truck Stops of America—servicing 1,000 vehicles a day—along with its rollicking Lucky Lady Lounge just next door.

Then I turned to look at my father's place, the Dallas Pike Truck Stop. When Interstate 70 was being constructed, he'd purchased 10 acres of hillside, intending to build one of the earliest truck stops along the highway. He soon discovered the sloping hill was all granite and essentially unbuildable. It took tons of dynamite and heavy-duty equipment to carve out a flat enough place to build his dream, and the result was a cheaply constructed concrete block building with a dozen uncovered gas pumps out front.

I entered the building and walked past the fuel desk, an enclosed space for the clerk and pump jockeys. Despite the "No Smoking" sign, the air inside it hung gray. The entrance to the restaurant, just beyond the fuel desk, was flanked by two poker machines strategically placed to tempt truckers to gamble away their hard-earned money.

I then stepped into the restaurant itself and saw waitresses serving plates heaped with steaks, burgers, bacon, pies, and gravy-smothered mashed potatoes. The booths, sheathed in plastic, were pockmarked by cigarette burns, and the tables were covered in stained cloths. To complete the look, the leaking roof had left rust-colored watermarks on the uneven ceiling tiles. And then I remember, as if on some cosmic cue, a waitress dropped a tray in the back of the restaurant, and the room filled with the earsplitting clatter of silverware and shattering plates.

Less than one week before, I had been performing complex brain surgery at a major university hospital and my father had been alive. In the weeks before that, I'd lived with my wife and two children in a lovely home. Now, looking out through dirty windows at black diesel fumes spewing from the big rigs, I was struck with a simple but extraordinarily loaded question: "How did I get here?"

AT GRUELING TIMES like this, when life leaves us absolutely reeling, it's common to think our horrible circumstances are a result of events that have happened *to* us. We can actually sense a physical pressure bearing down on us or feel as though we've been punched in the gut. And in fact, many things—the death of a loved one, news of a terrorist attack, or some natural disaster—are out of our control. I, however, would eventually face the

Less than one week before, I had been performing complex brain surgery at a major university hospital and my father had been alive. In the weeks before that, I'd lived with my wife and two children in a lovely home. Now, looking out through dirty windows at black diesel fumes spewing from the big rigs, I was struck with a simple but extraordinarily loaded question: "How did I get here?"

sickening realization that it had been personal choices that led me to that spot in the middle of a run-down truck stop, profoundly unhealthy in both the mental and physical sense. Other than my father's untimely death, my dire situation was the result of how I had, one conscious decision after another, allowed my life to career so precariously out of balance.

Yet Epictetus, a first-century philosopher who'd been born a slave, said, "It is not what happens to you, but how you react to it that matters," and this ancient adage still holds water today. In her book *The Myths of Happiness*, psychology professor Sonja Lyubomirsky explains how the choice of a positive attitude gives us options in any situation. "When bad things happen *to* us, it turns out that we have a lot more control over our realities than we believe."[1] She goes on to describe instances where people who faced bad news or a daunting task made a conscious decision to reframe their circumstances, and that's what defined their new reality. The recognition and appreciation of this power—that we can ultimately decide what we experience by choosing how to feel—is life altering.

It sounds so elegant and simple. Should be easy, right? But humans struggle mightily when it comes to adversity because when we're faced with weighty issues, our first reaction is often to blame external factors. I, for one, spent years heaping blame on others, on any outside force, in an attempt to wiggle out of responsibilities. My wife is expecting too much from me, I'd think; after all, I'm doing all this work to support my family. I can't eat well because of the lousy food in the hospital cafeteria. I'm so busy with work that I can't possibly exercise. Or spend more time with my children. Or attend church. Or get together with friends. Even when I knew I was making poor choices—really lousy choices—blaming things I perceived to be outside of my control relieved a great deal of pressure, and I felt safer behind my wall of rationalities.

Neuroscientist Joseph LeDoux, director of the Center for the Neuroscience of Fear and Anxiety in New York City, studies this clash between conscious knowledge on one side and emotional resistance and poor choices on the other in his seminal work, *The Emotional Brain*. The prefrontal cortex of our brain is the center for conscious decision-making, planning, personality expression, and behavior modification. The evolutionarily older amygdala, on the other hand, is the almond-sized structure in the temporal lobe that serves as the repository of all emotional experiences, particularly those associated with fear and anxiety. "While conscious control over emotions is weak," LeDoux writes, "emotions can flood consciousness. This is so because the wiring of the brain…is such that connections from the emotional systems to the cognitive systems are stronger than connections from the cognitive systems to the emotional systems."[2] Simply stated, in a wrestling match between our emotions and our intellect, our emotions will often pin us down for the count.

While I can rationally agree with the earlier quote by Epictetus—"It is not what happens to you, but how you react to it that matters"—this way of thinking is far easier with a healthy mind and the resilience to react appropriately to challenges. And at the time of my crisis, I had neither; countless poor choices had rendered me incapable of being self-aware, and my internal emotional battles were debilitating. I'd sunk into depression and had no hope that I could find my way back to a vibrant, balanced life. Yet I've come to feel nothing but sheer gratitude for that brutal experience, which served as the biggest wake-up call I could've received. In Father Richard Rohr's words, "Losing, failing, falling, sin, and the suffering that comes from those experiences—all of this is a necessary and even good part of the human journey."[3] Indeed, Rohr's book *Falling Upward* provides excellent proof that only by falling down do we truly understand getting up. ◻

Black and white

In a dialogue called "Phaedrus," the Greek philosopher Plato presented his famous allegory of the chariot to illustrate the conflict between intellect (the prefrontal cortex) and emotion (the amygdala). In it, the soul is a chariot that is driven by a human charioteer. Pulling the chariot are two winged horses—one white, the other dark.

The white horse, a "lover of honor," represents moral judgment and the rational mind. This horse has no need of the charioteer's whip; instead, it "is guided by word and admonition only." Its partner, however, is "shag-eared and deaf, hardly yielding to whip and spur," and represents the passions and irrational impulses so often tied to our emotions.

How can we as charioteers hold onto the reins of these disparate forces, which so frequently pull us in opposite directions? Plato explored this universal challenge and acknowledged it's a constant battle for the charioteer, who must often descend and try again.[4]

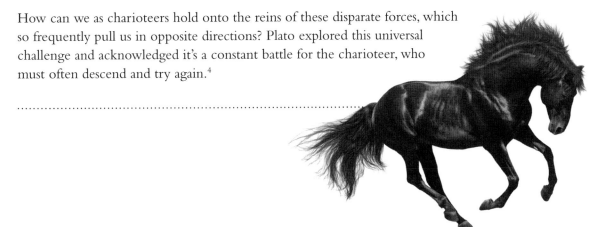

Out of Balance

The world is but a perpetual see-saw.

— French philosopher Michel de Montaigne

HOW DID I EXTRICATE MYSELF from this darkly comical situation? How did I reach the point where I could see this period as just a part of a larger journey? I wish it'd been as simple as walking out of that truck stop, signing a few papers to settle my father's estate, and then heading home to sort things out with my wife. But as is so often the case, things got much worse before they got better.

Both my body and my mind were reacting viciously to the stressors in my life, and I was in the grips of a profound depression. You probably already know that our bodies have hormones that start to flow when we are in stressful situations; both adrenaline, referred to as the "fight or flight hormone," and norepinephrine are produced almost immediately to provide a surge of energy so we can focus and take action. These two hormones, teamed with another stress hormone called cortisol, allow us to get through difficult or frightening situations and in some cases can actually save our lives.

When we face prolonged, unremitting stress, however, the adrenal glands go into overdrive to continuously release cortisol. And chronically elevated levels of this hormone can lead to everything from high blood pressure to headaches, sleep problems to cardiac irregularities, ulcers to acne. If the cortisol release continues, it can lead to depression and actual brain atrophy, or shrinkage. It also causes the death of brain cells, particularly those in the temporal lobes that serve memory.

In studies where rats are shocked but are allowed a degree of control—a lever they can press that decreases the intensity of the shock, for instance, or a passageway to escape their confines—their brains adapt and they can cope quite well. But in studies where rats are shocked at random and learn there's no action they can perform to avoid those shocks, something tragic happens: they give up. Their brains begin to atrophy, they lose their appetites, they no longer process sensory information, and they aren't able to regulate their own body temperatures. Eventually, the rats' bodies completely shut down.

The human brain is more advanced and more resourceful than a rat's, of course, and can usually solve complex problems and stay focused on longer-term goals. But depression does affect us in a similar way, and we can reach the same desperate point where our brains no longer function rationally. American existential psychologist Rollo May once defined depression as "the inability to construct a future,"[1] and I, for one, can attest to that dreadful

The link between brain and body

Neuroscientist Joseph LeDoux points out, "In emotions, unlike in cognition, the brain does not usually function independently of the body. Many if not most emotions involve bodily responses."[2] When we're sad, we may cry. When we're afraid, our heart rates go up and our pupils dilate. When we're calm, our heart rates go down and our breathing changes. It should come as no surprise, then, that severe depression can cause physical deterioration in the brain, suppression of our immune system, and damage to the blood vessels throughout our body. These are all examples of just how tightly the emotional mind and the physical body are linked.

28

experience. Overwhelmed by my past, paralyzed by my present, and unable to envision any way forward, I was in a terrifying place.

Another condition caused by chronically high levels of stress hormones is suppression of the immune system, a disruption of our body's natural ability to heal itself. Under normal circumstances, we're equipped to handle minor cuts and infections, we can stave off a cold, and we can easily repair things like a skin abrasion. When stress hormones are out of balance, however, our immunity essentially goes on strike; it simply has too many bigger things to worry about.

Again, I can personally attest to this downside of our biology because my own system did just that. Several months after I'd moved to Bridgeport, I was asked to take a part-time position at a local hospital. I performed only basic surgeries and was sending all major cases to Pittsburgh or other larger facilities. In one instance, however, the wife of a local physician presented with sudden severe headaches and deteriorating vision, and I knew I was dealing with a brain aneurysm. Her critical condition meant we couldn't transfer her to another hospital, so I took on the surgery and planned to seal off the aneurysm with a titanium clip. Toward the end of the procedure, however, I was struck with overwhelming nausea and chills. With no other surgeon available, I completed the operation but was then rushed immediately into the emergency room.

The whites of my eyes were yellow, and blood tests revealed my liver enzymes were off the charts. Combined with my other symptoms, I knew I'd contracted infectious hepatitis A, most likely from contaminated food at the truck stop. While a healthier body might have been able to fight the infection, my immune system had been compromised by my depression, and I took on every symptom of the disease: fatigue, muscle aches, headache, loss of appetite, low-grade fever, abdominal pain, nausea, vomiting—all of it.

Most people would have wisely stayed in the hospital, but not me. Why? Part of it was that I hated being sick; since I was the one trained to heal those in need, I felt uncomfortable relying on others. But my depression also made me withdraw, made me want to be alone rather than having to deal so directly with other people. For nearly three weeks, I stayed by myself in an old farmhouse on a piece of property my father had owned. My mother brought me soup and took care of me as much as I would let her, but I was otherwise isolated.

And as hard as it is now for me to acknowledge, I can say the third reason I didn't stay in the hospital was that I honestly didn't care what happened to me. I was so depleted, so hopeless, so utterly weighed down, that I thought dying would actually be better than living in such anguish. That is the ugliest side of depression.

The imbalance in my life had led to the deterioration of my health, which had then triggered what we now know are actual physical changes in the brain. All of this impacted my ability to work, meaning that I couldn't think as clearly, I couldn't stay focused, and I didn't have even a fraction of the interest or passion for my profession that I once had. Where I used to feel competent, I now felt inadequate. Where I once sought out challenges and welcomed difficult cases, I now felt an almost constant sense of dread. And while I once led teams of renowned colleagues, I was now avoiding the company of other people.

This is yet another casualty of the domino effect of stress and depression: relationships. When poor health knocks out your mental abilities, another inevitable element to topple is your ability to interact with others in a healthy, positive, meaningful way. My relationships at work suffered in the months leading up to my father's death; being in autopilot mode for so long had given me a flat affect and made me terse with my staff. And since I'd always been a very competitive person, my need for success had become an addiction over the years. I sought recognition from my peers rather than seeking ways to cooperate or collaborate with them, and in retrospect, that makes me terribly sad. I lost so many opportunities for connection and joy, and much of the time, I ended up competing brutally against myself. That makes for a very lonely game.

Automatic mode had also made me less compassionate with my patients. While I'd had a fine bedside manner in the earlier stages of my career, human beings had become patients and patients were merely cases. I can recall going out into a waiting room to talk to the large family of a woman who'd just died from a brain tumor. I explained the severity of the case and gave a few terse responses to their inquiries. Then I glanced at my watch. The

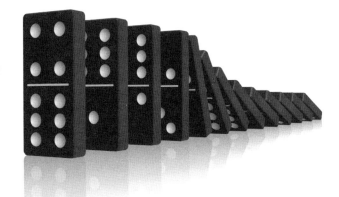

And that is yet another casualty of the domino effect of stress and depression: relationships. When poor health knocks out your mental abilities, another inevitable element to topple is your ability to interact with others in a healthy, positive, meaningful way.

patient's oldest daughter saw me and, with huge tears in her eyes, said, "We have questions. Can't you see we need you right now?" Her words stopped me cold. I'd been so detached, so arrogant—more worried about where else I needed to be—that I hadn't given this family what they needed from the doctor in the room: attention, compassion, and reassurance.

My stress and imbalance had certainly impacted my interactions with colleagues and patients, and the fact that my wife had taken our children and left me in the middle of a blizzard was a sure sign that they'd also affected my personal relationships. My wife and I had known each other well when we married, and for the first few years, everything felt solid and comfortable. When we had trouble conceiving children, we chose to adopt—first a son, and then a few years later, a daughter. As I moved through my residencies, however, I was spending more and more time at work, and my wife focused her attention on raising our children. I enjoyed the challenges of my work and reveled in the approval, recognition, and respect I got through my career. So although I knew we had an increasing disconnect at home, I didn't take any responsibility to acknowledge the problems, let alone make any effort to fix them. I simply backed off and redoubled my focus on my work.

I had unknowingly followed a precise recipe for how to destroy a marriage, using every ingredient caused by job burnout. (Little did I know that in 2015—35 years in the future—the Mayo Clinic would report that nearly 55 percent of doctors show symptoms

31

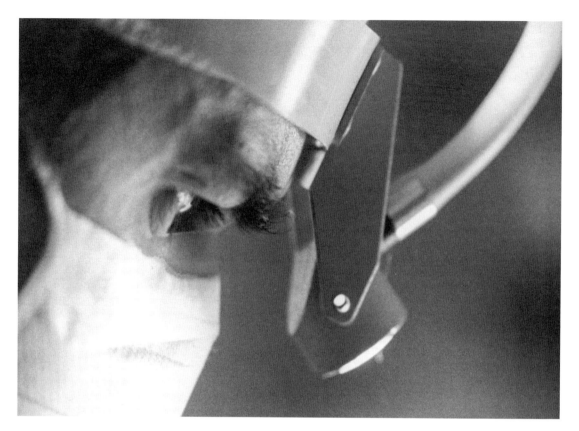

The photo above was taken in the operating room when I was clipping a complex aneurysm in a patient's brain. On the opposite page is a professional head shot from my early years as a neurosurgeon in Pittsburgh. And the photo on the left? That's the truck stop just outside of Wheeling, West Virginia, where I worked for nearly a year after my father's death.

"As a man thinketh in his heart, so is he." Had I ever thought with my heart? I'd been so consumed with the thinking I did in my head—the studying, the awards, the latest research, the next groundbreaking surgery—that I viewed thinking "from the heart" as weak. And now, even the thinking in my head was a mess.

of burnout, including emotional exhaustion, depersonalization, and a low sense of personal accomplishment. I wasn't alone, even back then, but it certainly felt that way.)[3]

Lying in bed in the farmhouse, the thoughts colliding in my head were that my health was terrible, my professional life had crumbled, and I had screwed up every single important relationship in my life. That bout with hepatitis was my nadir, and I'd sunk to the proverbial "rock bottom." In retrospect, the only good thing I managed to do during the weeks of the illness was to crack open a Bible—the well-worn, underlined, and dog-eared boyhood copy I used through over a decade of Catholic school education. In a fog of misery, I'd leafed through passages, looking for something—anything—to shed some light on my confusion. A passage like 2 Corinthians 12 certainly hit home: Paul is complaining about the thorn in his flesh and begging for God to take it out. God's reply? Hang in there; my grace is enough. Paul then realizes he must "delight in weaknesses, in insults, in hardships, in persecutions, in difficulties. For when I am weak, then I am strong." Could this adversity I was facing actually serve some good?

Or Proverbs 23:7, "As a man thinketh in his heart, so is he." Had I ever thought with my heart? I'd been so consumed with the thinking I did in my head—the studying, the awards, the latest research, the next groundbreaking surgery—that I viewed thinking "from the heart" as weak. And now, even the thinking in my head was a mess. The only thing that was clear was that my life needed to change, and in a very big way, if I wanted to survive. ◻

William Danforth and His Square

*But in the eyes of you, one of the priceless few,
I trust will come a gleam of battle as you read on. You can be
a bigger person and I am going to prove it to you.*

— William H. Danforth

IT MAY SEEM ODD that the founder of a company that produces wheat cereal and dog food would play any prominent role in a book about neuroscience and a balanced life. But William H. Danforth is not famous for any particular product he sold. Instead, he's best remembered for being a genuine, exemplary leader and a genius marketer, all because he understood people, how to support them, and how to motivate them. And he certainly motivated me during the most calamitous period of my life.

Less than a month after I'd recovered from hepatitis, I came across a slim, leather-bound book written by Danforth titled *I Dare You* on the shelf of my childhood bedroom. I'd received the book back in 1958 as a high school senior, part of a leadership prize from the Danforth Foundation, which had been set up by Danforth and his wife, Adda. When I lifted the cover, I saw where I'd signed my name, at the young age of 18, on the special bookplate inside. And then in the author's preface, I read these words:

"'I Dare You' is for the daring few who are headed somewhere. Those afraid to Dare might as well pass it up. It will weary the lazy because it calls for immediate action. It will bore the sophisticated, and amuse the skeptics....It will not be overly popular because it calls for courage swift and daring. But in the eyes of you, one of *the priceless few*, I trust will come a gleam of battle as you read on. You can be a bigger person and I am going to prove it to you."[1]

As mentioned in the previous chapter, depression causes drastic changes in the brain, so I'd felt dull and lethargic for months. Reading Danforth's words, however, triggered a profound response, a stirring that felt foreign and then comfortingly familiar. I devoured the rest of the book in one sitting and was incredibly moved by the message. To put *I Dare You* in context, however, it would help to know more about Danforth himself.

BORN IN 1870, William H. Danforth was raised in the swampy southeastern region of Mississippi County, Missouri, and was thin, frail, and sickly as a child. "Those were the days of chills and fever and malaria," he wrote. "When I came to the city to school, I was sallow-cheeked and hollow-chested."[2]

It was at school, however, that a passionate teacher named George Warren Krall looked Danforth right in the eyes and said, "I dare you to be the healthiest boy in the class. I dare you to chase those chills and fevers out of your system. I dare you to fill your body with fresh air, pure water, wholesome food, and daily exercise until your cheeks are rosy, your chest full, and your limbs sturdy."[3]

Danforth was so moved by this challenge that he did exactly what Mr. Krall told him to do, and for the rest of his life, he would equate living a full life with accepting the ultimate dare. He did become one of the physically strongest boys in his class and also excelled in his schoolwork, moving on to graduate from Washington University in St. Louis in 1892. Not long after that, he met Adda Bush, the woman who would be his wife for over 60 years, and began a company that mixed various feed for farm animals.

He was dedicated to his growing company and always looked for new, beneficial products to sell, for people as well as animals. Long before there was widespread knowledge about what constituted good nutrition, Danforth proclaimed the connection between diet and health. He worked with a miller to develop a cereal with the germ still intact, and he marketed the product under the name "Purina whole wheat cereal" because of its purity.

WILLIAM H. DANFORTH

A photo of me in high school, along with my copy of William Danforth's I Dare You, *which I'd received as a prize from the Danforth Foundation when I graduated in 1958. I'd glanced through the pages of the book just after receiving it, but I hadn't held the book in my hands or given any thought to its message in over 20 years. I could never have imagined that it would ultimately change my approach to living.*

At about the same time, the ideas of health advocate Albert Wester Edgerly, known as "Dr. Ralston," were becoming popular. Danforth asked Dr. Ralston to endorse his cereal, and by 1898, Danforth's company became known as Ralston-Purina.

While Danforth was the president of this successful business, he made sure his work commitments did not eclipse other areas of his life. He was a loyal husband and a devoted father to three children. He developed and nurtured countless professional relationships and personal friendships. And long before Fitbits and exercise routines, Danforth simply took a mile-long walk every morning and happily called himself a "faddist" about his health. "It pays," he wrote. "Good health has been the most profitable, most enjoyable fad I know."[4]

Danforth was also a religious man, but he didn't simply equate church attendance with a complete spiritual life. "Too much has been left to the preachers in the past," he wrote. "The day has gone when the radiant side of life can be located like a Sunday suit and only put on one day a week."[5] He asserted that a strong spiritual life helps to define a person's purpose, and that a spiritual foundation leads to happiness and fulfillment.

The many books he wrote to collect his thoughts included titles such as *Adventures in Achievement*, *As a Man Thinketh*, *Highlights from Europe*, and *Random Ramblings in India*. But his most memorable book—*I Dare You*—was originally published in 1938 in limited edition to be given out to family, friends, and business associates. The thin little book took off, though, and was soon in high demand from everyone—college counselors to preachers, business executives to organizations like the YMCA, "everyone whose aim it is to challenge men and women to superior accomplishment."[6]

Written as nothing short of a battle cry from an impassioned general to his determined troops, *I Dare You* was packed with personal anecdotes, strategies for better living, and a generous sprinkling of exclamation points and grammatically unnecessary capitalization. "I Dare You, who think life is humdrum, to start a fight,"[7] writes Danforth. About the lazy? "Rot!" he says, "I take issue with them."[8] And those who claim they have no opportunity to create? "Bosh!" Danforth decries. "Opportunities to create are popping out at you every minute of the day."[9]

The reader of *I Dare You* has no trouble hearing Danforth's voice on every page and can easily envision Danforth delivering his passionate words with a broad smile on his face. The man had achieved what he considered a balanced life because he valued four key areas: his health, his work life, his relationships, and his religious convictions. He kept a visual reminder of that all-important balance in the form of a square he referred to as his "checker": if his square's four sides were the same length and were "in check," he knew his life was shored and stable.

This interest in the square shape had begun just after Danforth started his feed business, when he was looking to package his products in some memorable way. He'd noticed how a family in his area always dressed in clothes made from the same red-and-white-checkered gingham, and he liked how he could identify the members of that family wherever they went. He began to package his various products in sacks decorated with a red-and-white-check pattern, and the original Ralston-Purina checkerboard "square" has become one of the most recognized logos in the world. In 1921, after learning a technique for pressing food from a European company, Danforth began producing square-shaped pellets of dog food that he dubbed "checkers." And then, in 1950, a cereal called Rice Chex—short for "checker" —was introduced. Its shape? A square.

I'D CERTAINLY READ my share of self-help books before, the kind filled with advice to "face your fears," "trust your feelings," and "be more efficient with your time." I would derive some benefit from each book and be motivated for a while, but because none of these books had truly resonated with me, I'd slip back into poor habits and conduct my life in the same old ways. But Danforth's book was decidedly different. It didn't coax or coddle me, and it didn't lay out some complicated grand plan. It just set forth the very logical idea that paying attention to how you spend your time ultimately defines how you spend your life. And it made sense. On page 21 of *I Dare You*, after Danforth explained the basics of his philosophy, he asked his readers, "Suppose you were to draw a picture of your life as you were living it today. How near four-square would it be?"[10]

So I followed Danforth's instructions and tried to draw my square according to how much time and effort I put into each of my four "sides." Having perfectionist tendencies and a strong desire to look good, I began muttering aloud, making excuses as I struggled to connect the four sides. I even took the time to locate a ruler, as if perfectly straight lines would somehow compensate for the imbalance. But after fifteen minutes of drawing, erasing, and self-loathing, I realized there was no way I could draw anything that even approximated a square. Exhausted, I finally got honest with myself and drew this:

work

physical   relationships

spiritual

My shape, if you could call it that, looked like some crude tool. Work was, of course, the lengthy handle, but the three sides on the right—illustrating my relationships, my spirituality, and my physical health—were ridiculously disproportional. My work had come to dominate my life, to the exclusion of everything else that deserved my attention. And I had no real awareness of, or insight into, how this had happened! It was a true epiphany to stare at this bizarre representation of my life, to look at this feebly unsquare "square," and recognize that my imbalance was the cause of my anguish. When I saw Danforth's example of an even four-sided square on the same page, I felt numb with regret. ◻

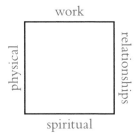

work

physical   relationships

spiritual

 In *I Dare You*, Danforth speaks directly to his readers, prompting them to reflect on their own lives and providing them with space to write down their goals. He even gives a dose of amusing tough love, asking "Will you listen to the little imps whispering in your ears that writing down the things you ought to do is merely piffle? Or will you put things down in black and white that need to be done and never quit until you can say 'Done!'?"[11] In keeping with Danforth's approach, I'm asking you to think about your own life as it is now.

1. In the space to the right, draw a shape that represents the four sides of your life as they are now, with the length of each side proportional to the time and effort you put toward that domain. Label the sides as *physical*, *work*, *relationships*, and *spiritual*.

2. Now do what Danforth suggested. Draw a square with four straight and equal sides, and label each side in the same order that you did above. Finally, write "My Checker" in the middle and sign it with your initials.

"No plan is worth the paper it is printed on unless it starts you doing something. There is too much telling in this life and not enough doing. Unless you have actually drawn and labeled your checker for yourself, even though the four-fold plan has only been outlined, you are not ready for the next step.

After you have drawn your checker, look at it well. Photograph it on your brain. There you have the picture of the Magic Square— the symbol of the richer, fuller life, the emblem you are to follow in your daring crusade."[12]

— William H. Danforth

43

First Steps

A round man cannot be expected
to fit into a square hole.
He must have time to modify his shape.

— Mark Twain

In April, just a few weeks after I'd drawn my lopsided square, an old acquaintance from Wheeling, Don Jebbia, called to ask if I'd like to go for a run with him at the high school track. Nothing could have sounded less appealing to me, but he was persistent. "C'mon, Joe," he said. "It'll be good for you."

I didn't know it at the time, but these were the truest words I would ever hear.

I found a pair of scuffed-up tennis shoes in the back of a closet and pulled on a pair of surgical scrubs and a sweatshirt. I hadn't run for several years, and it'd been over two decades since I'd done any training on that particular track, which happened to circle the field where I'd found success playing football. I later played in college and was named a Scholastic All-American, so I knew what it was like to train and be in tune with my own body. But on that day, I wasn't feeling in tune with anything.

I was middle-aged now and carrying about 20 pounds of excess weight, which on my small frame made a considerable difference. Even walking up a set of stairs had been leaving me short of breath. I was keenly aware, then, of how disconnected I was from my body; I moved awkwardly, couldn't find a comfortable pace, and had no breath control. Don, a fit and active runner, stayed right beside me, talking to me casually as we half walked, half jogged four quarter-mile laps around the track. When we stopped, I thanked Don for calling and went home, feeling even more miserable after my lousy performance. "Never again!" I thought.

That night, however, something remarkable happened: for the first time in months, I fell asleep easily and didn't wake up a single time during the night. The next morning, a light bulb could've been seen glowing over my head because I'd made a momentous connection that would change my life—*exercise could make me feel better.* I went back to the track alone and ran that day, and the day after that. And each day, I simply ran a little farther. Before a month was out, I'd moved from the high school track to the streets of the small town, and soon I was the "Forrest Gump" of Bridgeport, Ohio, running miles every day past the quaint houses and up into the hills of the Ohio Valley.

I also began to pay closer attention to what I was eating, cutting out the convenient junk food and calorie-laden fare from the truck stop and eating regular, balanced meals. I began drinking more water to keep my body hydrated and healthy. The pounds unintentionally fell away, but I didn't even bother counting them on the scale; I just knew my clothes fit differently, I could move with ease, and the strength returned to my muscles. When my knees and ankles began to ache, I learned about the relatively new event called the triathlon—a race involving running, biking, and swimming—and it made perfect sense to

*The next morning, a light bulb could've been seen glowing over my head because I'd made a momentous connection that would change my life—**exercise could make me feel better.** I went back to the track alone and ran that day, and the day after that. And each day, I simply ran a little farther.*

begin cross-training. Since the bicycle in my parents' garage had probably been purchased when I was in the eighth grade, I went out and bought a new one and soon saw how biking built up the antagonist muscles to those used for running. Within a few weeks, my joints were stronger and more balanced.

My next step was to ask the lifeguard at the local YMCA to teach me how to do a basic freestyle stroke. Up until then, I tended to sink when I swam any stroke other than the dog paddle. But I was so motivated by the possibility of competing in a triathlon that I listened carefully to his instructions and began doing laps. When I stopped fearing that I would drown, my breathing became more relaxed, and I built up the muscles necessary for swimming. In August, just four months after that first run with Don, I signed up for what's called a "Tin Man"—a 0.9-mile swim, a 25-mile bike race, and a 6.2-mile run. I didn't win the race, of course; in fact, I had to push myself the whole time to continue. But I felt such a profound sense of relief and accomplishment when I crossed the finish line that I knew prioritizing my health was the first step in reimagining a different life for myself.

Looking back on that first run with Don, I have to smile. While I'm sure he was concerned about me personally, he also happened to be the loan officer at the bank that held the mortgage on my father's properties. That little jog was a way for him to check in on me and make sure I'd be around long enough to pay off all those loans! Regardless of his motivation, I'm unspeakably grateful that he got me to that track and ran those first few laps next to me. Without a hint of hyperbole, I can say he redirected my entire life.

So what had happened? In January, I'd stood in the middle of a truck stop, depressed, alone, and in arrogant denial of how I could've possibly ended up in such a dismal situation. By March, I was so unhealthy that I was lying in bed nearly dead from an infection and so depressed that I had all but given up on finding happiness. But by the fall, I'd made a commitment to self-improvement and had completed a challenging triathlon. In the words of Charles Dickens, I felt "recalled to life."

High levels of cortisol, caused by stress and a complete lack of self-care, had led to depression, excess weight, and a host of other problems in both my body and mind. But exercise and an improved diet—which had the beneficial side effects of weight loss—had completely turned my life around. Rather than the knotted and gnarled mind-body connections that had sent me spiraling dangerously downward, my brain and my body were now working together, collaborating in a way that opened each up for improved function.

I've spent the first few chapters of this book telling a personal story of how the elements of my life became so fractured and broken that I had no firm foundation on which to stand. For me, lengthening and strengthening the physical side of my square first was essential because it proved to me that there were ways to take control of my life, that I could help myself *feel better* in every sense of the world—through my body, in my spirit and my brain, and in how I interacted with others. Chapter 5 will detail all of benefits of seeking a healthier body, which can be the foundation for a more balanced life. ❑

It's spelled t-r-i-a-t-h-l-o-n.

The first triathlon held in America took place in 1974 at Mission Bay in San Diego, and it attracted just shy of 50 participants. It consisted of a six-mile run, followed by five miles on a bike and a 500-yard swim. The men who conceived the idea—Jack Johnstone and Don Shanahan—even had to suggest to the trophy maker how to spell "triathlon" because it wasn't in any dictionary. Recounting his own difficulties in the race, Johnstone wrote, "As I dismounted my bike and tried to run, my legs felt like they didn't belong to my body. I let out a moan of anguish and remember someone yelling to me, 'Well, this was *your* idea!'" Founder Jack Johnstone writes that while they thought participants would finish in under an hour, many took almost twice that long. So with darkness descending, they arranged for a few cars to have their headlights illuminating the bay to allow the last few swimmers to finish the race.

At a reunion some 25 years later, organizers Don Shanahan (center) and Jack Johnstone (right) join Bill Phillips, who had won the first triathlon with a time of 55:44. These three men, along with several others involved in the Mission Bay races, were inducted into the Triathlon Hall of Fame in October of 1998.

49

Several years later, two of the race participants, husband and wife John and Judy Collins, organized the longer Ironman triathlon in Kona, Hawaii: a 2.4-mile swim, 112-mile bike race, and 26.2-mile marathon. Just over a dozen daring athletes took part in the first competition, but now Ironman races are held on six continents and draw thousands of elite athletes each year. Scott Tinley, a three-time Hawaiian Ironman champion, called it "the cruelest, baddest, toughest one-day show in all endurance sports!"[1] (And I could never have imagined when I struggled to finish that first Tin Man race that I would go on to complete the Ironman in Kona five times, and once each in New Zealand, Germany, and Canada!)

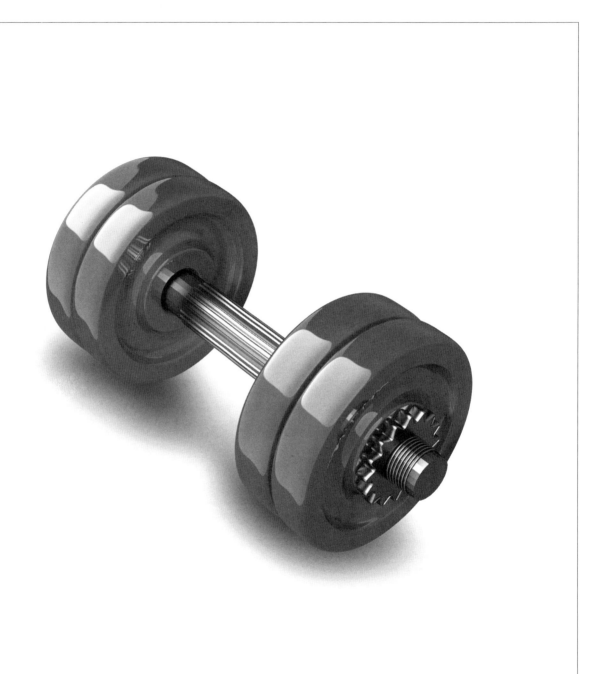

Body: The Physical Side

*It is difficult at first, but soon
the sheer joy of vigorous health amply rewards you
for daring to be strong and well.*

— William H. Danforth

IN 1979, the year I was taking that run around the track with Don, there was already an established link between exercise and better physical health. We knew "aerobic exercise," a term coined by Dr. Kenneth Cooper in 1968, was good for the heart, improved lung capacity, and helped regulate blood pressure.[1] It also strengthened muscles, kept bones healthy, and allowed for more flexible joints. I was indeed part of the running revolution that began in the 1970s, and I could feel these benefits: I was considerably stronger, I was sleeping better, and my excess pounds had come off as the unintended—and very welcome—consequence of more physical activity.

In addition to these long-known perks of regular exercise, more recent research proves that exercising increases our longevity because it affects the body on a cellular and chemical level. Consistent activity boosts immunity and tamps down inflammation—the common denominator of heart disease, cancer, Alzheimer's, and other serious health issues. By reducing the amount of time food spends in the digestive system, exercise decreases the risk of colon cancer; by lowering hormone levels in older women, it may help decrease the chance of developing breast cancer. And exercise even affects our very DNA. Every chromosome in our body, for instance, is capped on both ends with telomeres, which protect the genetic data in the chromosome much like a plastic tip protects a shoelace from fraying. As we get older, these telomeres shorten, and the rate of their shortening is linked to the pace of aging, an increased tendency for depression, and a greater chance of developing certain types of cancer. Studies now suggest that exercise delays the shortening of these telomeres, thus prolonging their important function.[2] Just think of *that* the next time you tie up the laces of your walking shoes!

Exercise also has significant benefits to the brain. When I began running regularly back in Bridgeport, Ohio, my depression lifted and I felt more focused than I had in years. The very concept of a mind-body connection dates back to ancient times, suggested by how the philosopher Plato advised the Greeks to "avoid exercising either mind or body without the other, and thus preserve an equal and healthy balance between them." And the teachings of Buddha included the warning, "To keep the body in good health is a duty….Otherwise, we shall not be able to keep our mind strong and clear."

Early on, however, the nascent fields of science and medicine couldn't find evidence to support any link between the mind and the body. When sixteenth-century scientists

Our bumpy brains

Scientists have made some really inaccurate hypotheses about the mysterious gray matter in our skulls over the years. Yet some of these wacky ideas led to the modern tools so critical to understanding and ultimately helping the human brain. One off-the-wall pseudo-science was phrenology, a theory popularized in the eighteenth century by German physician Franz Josef Gall, who claimed bumps on our skulls revealed our mental faculties. He was quite wrong about the bumps but correct that our emotions, thoughts, and abilities stem from localized parts of the brain.

ignored church rules and secretly dissected corpses to learn about anatomy, for example, all the organ systems they identified seemed to reach a dead end at the base of the skull. Imagine the frustration of those early physicians when they looked at the wrinkled, gelatinous gray matter inside the skull! None of their attempts to cut and explore offered up any helpful answers, so without the ability to pinpoint the source of emotions, scientists began to dismiss their importance. By the seventeenth century, Frenchman René Descartes, a key figure in the Scientific Revolution, ranked rational thought above all else. In *The Balance Within: The Science Connecting Health and Emotions*, author Esther Sternberg, MD, writes, "In Descartes' orderly division of the world into rational and irrational—provable and unprovable—emotions and their relationship to health and disease clearly fell into the latter domain. And there they remained until scientific tools powerful enough to challenge the categorization could rescue them."[3]

What exactly were these tools? Considerable advances over the last few decades—in anatomy, neurochemistry, brain mapping, and other technologies—have revealed many of the exciting secrets of the brain. We now have fMRI (functional magnetic resonance imaging), for example, along with PET scans (positron emission tomography) and SPECT scans (single-photon emission computed tomography) to detect connections between blood flow to the brain and activity within specific brain cells. This allows us to track brain activity on a computer screen in 3-D, to actually see where emotions such as anger, joy, fear, and sadness are generated at the precise moment they're experienced. All of this advancement means the gray matter that baffled early scientists is now much less baffling. We now know both our emotions and our cognitive abilities are localized in specific areas of the brain— the core of the central nervous system—so there are undeniable connections between our feelings, our thoughts, and our mental and physical health.

As we uncover more about the brain, information pours into health magazines, medical journals, news sources, websites, and blogs. From "The ten best brain foods!" and "A supplement to guarantee clearer thinking!" to endless options for dieting to lose weight, we are bombarded with messages—very few that can bear scrutiny. To reduce the confusion,

I'll look briefly at four areas of brain research that highlight the incredible importance of the physical side of Danforth's square. These areas are neurogenesis, endocannabinoids, epigenetics, and nutrigenomics.

Neurogenesis: A whole new brain

When I was in medical school, doctors were taught that organs like the heart and liver could regenerate cells, but that the brain could not: everyone started with roughly 100 billion brain cells at birth, and when those were gone, they were gone. In 1998, however, collaboration between Fred H. Gage, a professor of genetics at the Salk Institute in California, and Peter Eriksson, a professor of neurology at Sweden's Göteborg University, revealed otherwise. After mapping the brains of mice using radioisotopes, they sent the mice "to the gym" and had them run on a wheel. Researchers remapped their brains and found increased cell proliferation and cell survival, while mice kept inactive over the same time period showed no new brain cells. And the most significant growth was in the hippocampus, the brain area associated with memory and most damaged by depression. Proving this process—this neurogenesis, from the Greek for "the birth of neurons"—was revolutionary. Gage and his associates later demonstrated that this process also occurs in humans and that the human hippocampus retains its ability to generate neurons over the course of a lifetime.[4]

And the main player in the amazing process of neurogenesis is a particular protein called BDNF (brain-derived neurotrophic factor). The Greek *trophe* means "nourishment," so BDNF is a superfood—a kind of Miracle-Gro for the brain—responsible for everything from developing those new brain cells to working magic in the frontal cortex, where it helps the brain with focus, abstract thinking, and decision making. And BDNF is also busy encoding memories, enhancing the plasticity or flexible thinking in our brains, and maintaining the axons and synapses that form the highways between nerve cells.

When I was at my lowest point and suffering from depression with a tired, unfocused brain, my neurogenesis was compromised. Modern MRIs of patients with depression now reveal that brain cells are destroyed and not replaced, and in severe cases, a region of the brain called the dorsolateral prefrontal cortex actually shrinks, causing difficulties with memory, sensory integration, and planning. Although the antidepressants I was initially prescribed helped in the short term—we now know they were increasing the production of BDNF—my choice to continue exercising is what allowed for long-term benefits once I stopped taking the medication. Indeed, Duke University conducted studies on three groups of people with depression, one group treated with drugs, the second treated with drugs and put on an exercise program, and the third placed only on an exercise program. Ten months later, the group that had focused only on exercise was the most successful in maintaining wellness and avoiding relapse.[5]

Endocannabinoids

The study of endocannabinoids is the next logical field to explore because it also relates to the positive feelings I had when I began running. In addition to increasing the production of BDNF and "feel good" brain neurotransmitters like dopamine, serotonin, and endorphins, my consistent exercise was also releasing anandamide, the body's natural version of the chemical compounds found in marijuana. First identified in 1992 by Raphael Mechoulam at Israel's Hebrew University of Jerusalem, anandamide can block pain and depression and improve mood. Taken from the Sanskrit word *ananda*, "bliss," it is now seen as one of the natural chemicals related to the "runner's high"—a sense of euphoria and peace that can be achieved while exercising —and is often referred to as the "bliss compound."

When scientists first began studying marijuana, they found that tetrahydrocannabinol (THC), the chemical responsible for the drug's psychological effects, binds to chemical receptors in the brain that regulate functions such as mood, memory, pain, anxiety, and sleep. Unlike cocaine, heroin, or other opiates, the THC didn't significantly affect dopamine—the main chemical in the brain's "reward system"—and therefore may not lead to the same level of addiction. But THC can calm stress, reduce pain, and improve mood, which is why marijuana is sometimes considered as a medical adjunct treatment for the pain, depression, and low appetite associated with cancer.

Exercise is powerful medicine

Between 1999 and 2012, the percentage of Americans taking antidepressants rose from just under 7 percent to 13 percent.[6] While up to 70 percent of those taking antidepressants respond with a reduction of symptoms, the long-term depression recurrence rate for patients who were only treated with drugs can be as high as 50 percent. In addition, the side effects of these drugs can be profound: fatigue, nervousness, insomnia, low sexual desire and sexual dysfunction, and weight gain are all common.

What about a solution for depression that offers the same benefits, but lasts beyond any drug treatment plan and requires no prescription? And not only does this solution avoid the side effects of many antidepressant drugs, it actually gives us more energy, makes us more relaxed, helps us sleep better, encourages more intimacy, and helps us lose weight.

We do have that solution: physical exercise. In numerous head-to-head studies, regular physical exercise of just 30 minutes a day was significantly better in lessening symptoms of depression in both the short and long term as compared to antidepressant drugs.

A photo of me on the bike leg of the Muncie 70.3 in July of 2016. The lake swim, bike portion, and run cover a total of 70.3 miles, half the distance of an Ironman. I was able to finish first in my age division and am considering taking on the full Kona Ironman in 2017.

Exercise allowed me to tap into my own personal pharmacy, located in my brain and offering a dazzling array of healing compounds—legal in all states and completely free. Because more positive chemicals were being released, my hypothalamus was no longer compromised and could go about doing its job of maintaining physiological and neurochemical homeostasis or balance within my body and brain. After being so unhealthy for so long, my body had finally regained a status quo across all my systems—from hunger and sleep to blood pressure, heart rate, and emotional control.

Epigenetics: Our genes are not our destiny

If an explanation of neurogenesis and endocannabinoids isn't enough to convince us to take care of our health, there's another exciting field of neuroscience—epigenetics ("in addition to or above genetics")—that also plays a key role in our overall wellness.

You probably learned in biology class that DNA, first identified in 1953, is considered a recipe book that holds the instructions for making all of the proteins in our bodies. And you were likely told that genes, the distinct stretches of DNA, determine everything about us: our height, hair, eye and skin color, athleticism, how we respond to environmental triggers, and so much more. Since genes are the molecular units of heredity passed from parent to offspring, our genes were considered our destiny—the concept of "genetic determinism." My own father died at the age 60, so for many years, I thought there was little I could do to avoid the same genetic time limit.

Just like the long-held belief that brain cells don't regenerate, however, this notion has also been debunked. We now know that only about 30 percent of our genetic code falls into the "determined" category, which means the remaining 70 percent is actually under our control. The revolutionary new understanding of this 30/70 ratio is the basis of the field of epigenetics, a study of how diet, stress, exercise, and environmental factors (such as pesticides, pollutants, and heavy metals) affect our genes without altering their actual structure. In short, it is possible to flip "switches" on or off in roughly 70 percent of our genes, either for a more positive result or to our detriment.

Through the findings of epigenetics, we can confidently say that up to 70 percent of the diseases we acquire—like cancer, heart disease, arthritis, diabetes, and Alzheimer's disease— are directly related to the choices we make.

To explain epigenetics with an easily understood metaphor, American biologist and epigenome pioneer Dr. Randy Jirtle relates it to technology. If the genome, the sum of all of our genetic material, is the hardware of a computer, he explains, "the epigenome would be like the software that tells the computer when to work, how to work, and how much." Dr. Jirtle's 2003 experiments on mice and their offspring produced staggering results: he was able to alter the color of their coats, their weight, and their susceptibility to disease by changing their diet.[7]

Through the findings of epigenetics, we can confidently say that up to 70 percent of the diseases we acquire—like cancer, heart disease, arthritis, diabetes, and Alzheimer's disease—are directly related to the choices we make. By rearranging a person's epigenetic tags or switches, which activate genes or shut them down, epigenetics has the potential to forge revolutionary new approaches to obesity, longevity, and disease. To a large degree, then, we can play boss to our genes, altering them for the better through diet, exercise, and stress control and by avoiding harmful environmental factors.

Nutrigenomics: Feeling great in our genes

While twentieth-century nutritional science was primarily concerned with identifying vitamins and minerals and with preventing diseases caused by nutrient deficiency, nutrigenomics goes much deeper. Aided by significant advances in genetic research, scientists can now understand how certain nutrients affect the systems of our bodies on a molecular level. Nutrients are not only building blocks for our cells but also switch epigenetic tags on or off, for better or for worse, so the food we choose has an undeniable impact on our genome and therefore on our health.

In my case, not only had I neglected physical exercise during the years leading up to my depression, but I'd also ignored everything I knew about good nutrition. I'd skip breakfast, grab packaged foods for their convenience, never consider the value of ingredients, overeat while traveling, and come home too late from work to eat a healthy meal with my family. And later, at my father's truck stop, the food was even worse. I was eating burgers consisting of hormone- and antibiotic-infused beef, fatty nitrate-laden bacon, and mystery sausage on buns made of bleached white flour. The french fries were cooked in trans-fatty acids and covered in salt. The sodas I'd drink were nothing but phosphoric acids, artificial additives, and high fructose corn syrup. And I was eating these things every day.

When nutrients are digested in our systems, the body releases molecules called transcription factors. These factors enter our cells and pass into the nuclei—where nearly six-foot-long strands of DNA are spooled into every living cell—and deliver information about the recently acquired nutrients. The research of nutrigenomics shows that by tripping the genes' regulation switches in the DNA, the transcription factors enable genetic instructions to play out, with either healthy or unhealthy outcomes. The kind of fast-food diet I was eating, like the one that has unfortunately become a staple for so many people, is interpreted as nothing short of an assault by those transcription factors. When DNA receives information about such poor nutrition, inflammatory proteins are triggered to counteract the assault, and over time, this damages our blood vessels, our brains, our livers, our skin, and our joints. And every time we accumulate 3,500 calories and don't burn them off? It becomes another pound of fat, which is only more bad news for our bodies.

What's become known as the Western diet is a lot of processed food, and the more processed a food is, the further it is from a nutritious whole food. This can all be traced back to the rolling mills of the 1860s that produced refined white flour, and to the booming sugar trade that followed. Team that with refined oils, the invention of high fructose corn

In the last 150 years, our food has changed more than it had over the last 10,000 years, and our health has suffered from it: obesity, chronic diseases, forms of cancer linked to diet, and type 2 diabetes are all on the rise.

syrup, and the development of modified foods that contain countless chemicals and dyes, and we've ended up with a diet that quite literally makes us sick. In the last 150 years, our food has changed more than it had over the last 10,000 years, and our health has suffered from it: obesity, chronic diseases, forms of cancer linked to diet, and type 2 diabetes are all on the rise.

The answer to this chaos? First is constraint, which is about minimizing our reliance on food as comfort or entertainment, and celebrating it instead as our life source. Second is a return to whole foods like vegetables, fruits, nuts, whole grains, legumes, olive oil, and seafood, along with lean proteins from poultry, eggs, cheese, and dairy in moderation— referred to as the Mediterranean diet. Third is recognizing how much added sugar we consume and knowing that our bodies are simply not designed to metabolize an excessive amount. We also need lots of water for essential hydration, and flavorful herbs and spices to reduce the need for added salt. For those who drink alcohol, a moderate amount of red wine provides ideal antioxidants, including resveratrol, for the heart.

We are bombarded with diet advice from every conceivable source. The bottom line is simply that whole foods trigger the production of anti-inflammatory proteins, switch on the right genes for optimum health, and don't contain the empty calories that lead to obesity. This reasonable approach to food—teamed with physical exercise—lengthened and strengthened the physical side of my square at a critical time in my life, and an ongoing commitment has kept me in excellent health well into my 70s. ◻

On the next few pages, I offer ideas to get you thinking about lengthening and strengthening the physical side of your square, as well as specific ways to take action. Don't skip over this section; these pages will be the most important in the whole book if they can motivate you to make the changes necessary to get and stay healthier.

Keep a food journal

You've likely heard this advice before, but—truly—the only way to learn about making good nutritional choices is to see what you're eating now. No need to tally up calories at this point; you're simply getting an idea of current habits. For a full week, write down or use an electronic device to capture what and how much you're eating, along with the time and place.

Time	Location	What I Ate
7:30 a.m.	Coffee shop	Coffee with cream and sugar, large blueberry muffin
9:30 a.m.	Work	Banana and a bowl of potato chips from staff room
12:15 p.m.	Deli near work	Cream of chicken soup, large soda, ham sandwich

At the end of the week, go back through and note any trends. Are you in the habit of eating a healthy breakfast? Do you snack in front of the television? How many times did you eat out at a restaurant compared to eating at home? What kind of liquids did you drink?

Keep track of your sleep, too

While you're noting what you've eaten, also keep track of when you go to bed and when you wake up. Experts differ on the exact number of hours of recommended sleep, but they all agree that consistent sleep/wake times are key. Adults should aim for between 7½ and 9 hours of sleep and should recognize that getting less rest on a regular basis can lead to health problems.

Once you've determined a baseline of your nutrition and sleeping habits, consider getting a fitness app or an activity tracker so you have all of this important data in one place.

Cultivate a healthy mindset

An inaccurate mindset may be hindering your health. Try reading the following statements aloud to get a sense of your way of thinking.

Common mindset:
My goal is to lose weight.

Better mindset:
My goal is to be healthy. Losing weight just happens to be a great side effect of choosing better health. When I focus only on losing weight, the process becomes about a diet or short-term exercising. By focusing on being healthy, I begin to understand what it takes to lengthen and strengthen the physical side of my square.

Common mindset:
I deserve to eat rich, calorie-heavy foods; they are my "rewards."

Better mindset:
Eating certain foods—a bag of chips, a sundae, a 500-calorie coffee drink—may feel like a reward, but it lasts for minutes. My true reward is to be able to revel in all the things good health can offer me today and for the long term. Remember: *Nothing tastes as good as healthy feels.*

Common mindset:
I want to get healthy, but it's just too hard.

Better mindset:
I have no excuses for not making healthier choices.

In Dan Pink's *A Whole New Mind*, he suggests getting rid of "buts" by rewriting negative statements. "I'd like to eat better, but I'm surrounded at work by sugary snacks" becomes "I'd like to eat better, and I'm surrounded at work by sugary snacks. So I'll pack my own supply of more healthful stuff to reduce my temptation to eat the bad stuff." He explains that "exchanging *and* for *but* can move you out of excuse-making mode and into problem-solving mode. It's grammar's way of saying, 'Deal with this.'"[8]

Think about what you're eating

Check off the foods that are a regular part of your diet, meaning you eat them at least several times a week.

___ white rice and pasta
___ crackers
___ sugar cereals
___ deli meats
___ fried foods
___ creamy dressings
___ fast food
___ soda (diet or regular)
___ frozen meals
___ sweetened yogurts
___ pork products
___ frozen or restaurant-style pizza
___ potato chips and pretzels
___ white potatoes
___ full-fat ice cream
___ candy

___ Greek yogurt
___ blueberries, strawberries, raspberries
___ lean chicken and turkey
___ seafood
___ nuts
___ brown rice, quinoa, and whole wheat pasta
___ sweet potatoes
___ broccoli and cauliflower
___ green tea
___ oatmeal
___ herbs, spices, and garlic
___ spinach and kale
___ avocados
___ beans and lentils
___ olive oil
___ eggs

If you regularly eat items from the left column, you're putting processed foods into your body that contain added sugar, excessive sodium, artificial chemicals, and unhealthy trans fats. If you routinely choose from the items listed on the right, you're eating whole foods that provide the vitamins, minerals, proteins, and energy you need to stay healthy.

Healthy people get into a routine, relying on 20 to 30 key whole-food ingredients like those listed on the right. They'll choose from perhaps three or four different breakfast and lunch items, know what constitutes a healthy snack, and have a dozen or more go-to dinners in their repertoire. This effortless approach to balanced eating allows their bodies to expect good nutrients at regular intervals, which is the key to long-lasting health.

Take a look in your refrigerator and pantry to gauge how many whole-food items you have compared to how many processed products you have. A commitment to buy more whole foods and master a few simple, healthy recipes isn't a "diet." Instead, it transforms how you eat.

Adjust to new habits

Getting used to new habits requires some time. If you've kept a food log and a sleep log, it'll be easy to see where you can make improvements, and the process will come more naturally if you adopt these changes one at a time. Stick with the new habit for a few weeks and then add another good habit. What kind of good habits am I talking about?

- Drink more water. Buy a great water bottle and keep it filled up. Every system in your body depends on staying hydrated—including your hair, skin, digestive system, and muscles—and water carries nutrients to your cells. Soda, diet soda, energy drinks, and artificially sweetened teas are all liquids, but their excessive sugar and lack of nutrients make them a poor choice.

- Don't keep junk food in your house or desk drawer. If it's not an option, you won't be tempted by it. Simplify your choices by having healthy food at your fingertips.

- Don't eat anything after you've eaten dinner. This doesn't mean you go to bed hungry. It means you go to bed with an emptied stomach. If you go to bed with food that still needs to be digested, you'll have more restless sleep and your body can't focus on what it's supposed to do during the night—like repairing cells, resting its complex systems, and converting new information to long-term storage in your brain.

- Eat breakfast. Every morning. You will not lose weight by skipping breakfast; in fact, eating breakfast wakes up your metabolism and gives your body the proper energy it needs. And people who eat a good breakfast are much less likely to overeat later in the day.

- Get more sleep. If you're not getting the recommended amount of sleep, aim to go to bed 10 minutes earlier each night for several nights until you reach a healthier bedtime. And shutting off the television and other screen devices at least an hour before bedtime will help you fall asleep more easily and have more restful sleep.

Exercise

My own experience taught me that my poor health—both mental and physical—was due in large part to my poor choices. Once I began eating better foods and exercising, I literally changed my life. Simply put, you can't "out exercise" a lousy diet, so if you're struggling with your health, you must begin by putting better food in your body. Then explore ways to make movement part of your daily life.

- Take the stairs.
- Park your car far away from the door.
- Meet friends at a park rather than at a restaurant.
- Find a place to walk during your lunch hour.
- Do push-ups and sits-ups every morning.
- Dance in your living room.
- Do charity walks and fun runs.
- Exercise while you watch television.
- Clean your house with high energy.
- Move and play with your kids.
- Try a yoga class.

65

" The line of least resistance makes for crooked rivers and crooked men. Each fish that battles upstream is worth ten that loaf in lazy bays. True, the mass of people prefer the easy way. Old ways require no effort. Physically or mentally lazy people do not want to adjust themselves. But they have never tasted the thrill of victory."[9]

— William H. Danforth

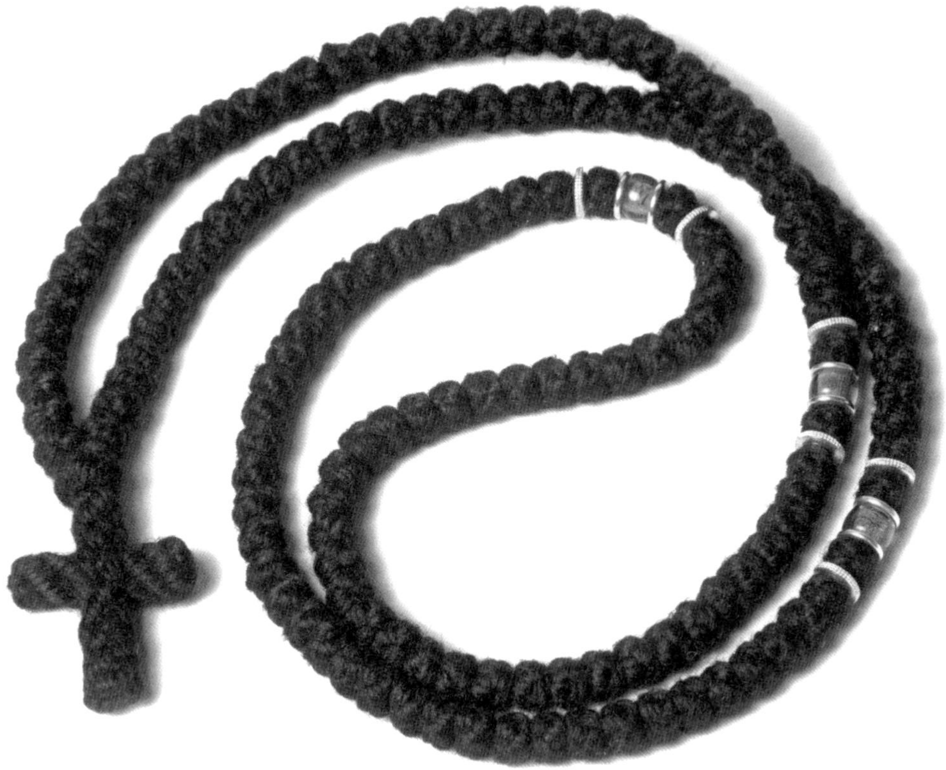

Soul: The Spiritual Side

It is to you, strong of body, brilliant of mind, magnetic of personality, that I am talking now. What price are all of these without the inspiration of a Cause?

— William H. Danforth

IN ADDITION TO ADDRESSING the physical side of my square during my time in Ohio, I had also begun to consciously focus on regaining a connection to my spiritual life. Passages from the Bible had comforted me during my lonely battle with hepatitis, and after reading Danforth's *I Dare You*, I'd been inspired by his unwavering commitment to be more mindful and to maintain his focus on developing consistent, positive habits. Although he was a practicing Christian, Danforth did not focus solely on Christianity in his book but instead addressed the broader need to build character through living a purposeful life. "It is the spirit that naturally makes you do the right thing at the right time," he wrote.[1]

And for his readers who may think developing a spiritual side is just another burden to bear? Something they *should* do or *have to* do? He advised, "If you consider the building of character, or ethics, or morals, or religion—whatever you choose to call it—as an opportunity to grow, then the unseen things of life take on a new significance."[2]

At the time, I knew I needed to do more "right things" in my life and to reconsider the entire notion of "significance" and "purpose." So even though I couldn't remember the last Sunday I'd attended mass, the habits of my Catholic upbringing sent me off to confession.

When I reached out to our neighborhood church, I was told a visiting priest from Nigeria was available. At first, it felt awkward sharing something this personal. But I quickly forgot my audience, and in the darkened confessional, everything came pouring out. My confession even included an animated description of Danforth's concept of a four-sided way of life, which I'm sure baffled the priest. When I'd finally finished, completely spent, the voice on the other side of the confessional wall said, in a crisp melodic accent, "You must say six Hail Marys and eight Our Fathers"—and then suggested some community service!

I walked home with a smile on my face, the first in a very long time, not because I'd experienced any great religious epiphany but simply because I'd been able to step back from my own emotional mess and begin to analyze it. For so long, I was completely caught up by negativity—exhaustion, competition, guilt, hopelessness, doubt, fear—and those negative feelings were so pervasive that they simply became my normal. The act of confessing was very cathartic and had allowed me to bring all of the painful feelings to the surface, to realize how abnormal and undesirable they really were. My father had often advised me to "look and really see, to listen and really hear," but only after hitting the proverbial rock bottom was I able to see the selfish, unkind decisions I'd made and to replay—and finally hear—the painful dialogues I'd had with those I hurt.

In 2010, I had the honor of providing medical help to Father Joseph Ephraim, an archimandrite in the Greek Orthodox Church. He presented me with the prayer rope seen on page 66, and I now wear it around my neck every time I perform surgery. I can feel its weight as I work, and it reminds me of Father Ephraim's faith and the calmness he radiates.

I was left raw and uncovered after that confession, yet I also felt indescribable relief because I knew lengthening and strengthening the spiritual side of my square would allow me to finally find an honest purpose in my life, which I'd always managed to marginalize.

A GOAL OF ALL SPIRITUAL PRACTICE—whether it's worship, yoga, community service, prayer, or meditation—is to gain perspective on the greater purpose of our lives, and these practices may well provide the best answers we have to the very large question of "Why?" Author and business expert Simon Sinek explores this concept, not through Danforth's favorite square shape, but through the equally simple circle. In his book *Start With Why*, he presents three concentric circles: the outside ring is labeled "what," the middle ring "how," and the inside circle "why." He goes on to explain that while most organizations can easily identify their *whats* and *hows*, they often don't address the most critical element: *why*.

"By why, I mean what's your purpose, what's your cause, what's your belief?" Sinek explained in a TED Talk in 2009. He says it's straightforward and relatively easy to start on the outside because *what* and *how* are objective ideas. Yet the most successful companies— and the most fulfilled people—have figured out that it is much more valuable to move in the opposite direction, beginning with the difficult *why* at the core and moving outward.[3]

Before my year in Wheeling, I had always remained focused on the *whats* and *hows* in my life, preferring those to more subjective, "fuzzy" ideas like purpose; I kept my eyes on the prize, as they say. I even became a doctor without any particularly mindful choice. As the first child on either side of my family to go to college, my father expected me to be an attorney. Although I was on a football scholarship at Indiana University, I suspect my good grades in high school led me to being housed in a dorm with many premed students. Several of these friends encouraged me to consider medicine, and I took up the challenge, getting accepted into medical school after my third year of college. Did I study hard and take my role seriously? Absolutely. Was I good at neurosurgery? It turns out I was. But again, I was driven primarily by *whats* and *hows*—information, technique, research, technology, reviews, and all the other tangible skills required of a doctor—rather than by any true, deep sense of *why*.

And this was also how I routinely approached other areas of my life. Physically, I'd always trained to look fit and to keep up with everyone else on the football field or squash court, but I'd never really appreciated the process of training and the value of teammates, or considered the joyous benefits of good health. I'd gotten married during my last year of medical school without authentic enough reasons, either. I sensed it was the right time and that marriage was something I should do, so while my first wife was a lovely, dynamic woman and later a wonderful mother, I didn't treat her or our family with enough respect or mindful purpose.

Even my approach to religion hadn't allowed for enough *why*. As a child, my family and I attended church regularly, and twelve years of nuns and Bible classes in a Catholic school reinforced a sense of gravity about religion. But I never explored the beauty and practices of other religions or stepped back to see the true benefits of connecting to larger purposes and ideas. So when I fell out of the routine of attending church after I began medical school, the importance of religion fell away, too. In short, I never invested the time it takes to wrestle with the complex, personal issues of the *whys* of my life—my work, my health, my relationships, or my spirituality. So does it come as any real surprise that I felt so unbalanced? It was truly just a matter of time before the *whats* and *hows* eroded away and exposed the fact that I was living my life without any deep sense of purpose.

While depression can lead many into darker and darker places, I am profoundly grateful that my depression ultimately helped to make me more appreciative of all my life experiences that were to follow. While it took time for me to figure it out, I eventually realized that my *why* was to help others. Yes, I was familiar with the Hippocratic oath and had always been committed to being good at my job. Yet I'd spent the vast majority of the time viewing the role of a physician from my perspective—my ego, my accolades, my accomplishments— and it had left me empty. When I turned the role around and finally saw what I could do for others, however, my *why* became clear. My skills put me in the incredible position of being able to improve people's lives—and in many cases to save their lives—and I learned to respect and be grateful for those skills, rather than attach a sense of entitlement to them.

I've also continued to find great comfort in learning about varied religious and spiritual practices, and while I embrace all the benefits of modern science, I respect the deeply held human need for belief in something that cannot be seen or explained. I repeat simple mantras and Bible passages in my mind while I'm running miles, swimming laps, or biking hills to train for races, and I have no doubt those words help me get through grueling competitions. I also take the time to learn about my patients' lives, their families, and their concerns, and if they wish, I'll touch their hand or arm and say a simple prayer with them. I can see the calming effect immediately—in their faces, in their eyes, in their grip on my hand. And numerous studies have shown that by embracing faith when dealing with medical procedures, patients have lower stress-related cortisol levels, improved immune systems, and even reduced recovery time.[4]

ONE OF THE MOST INSPIRING people I have ever met is an ideal example of someone who not only found but then wholly embraced his *why*. Rajesh Durbal, the son of Indian parents living in Trinidad and Tobago, was born in 1979 with major congenital deformities of his right arm and both of his legs. Before he was a year old, his legs were amputated just below the knees, and he spent three months in a full-body cast after surgery to fuse several of his bones. Raised by his loving family in New York City, Rajesh spent much of his younger years in and out of hospitals and trying new prosthetics to improve his mobility. But he was brutally teased by his peers, so Rajesh hid in long sleeves and baggy pants and shied away from the stares. "There were so many times that I just dreaded going to school," he says. "I dreaded the whispers, dreaded trying to keep up with everyone."[5]

His family continued to challenge him physically—his father insisted he learn to drive a stick-shift car—and reminded him there was nothing wrong with his brain. Rajesh, however, fell in with the wrong crowd in high school, smoked and experimented with drugs to "fit in," and gave little thought to his health. "I had so many emotions, so many painful feelings, and no insight into what my future could look like," he says. "It's still hard to talk about it, but there were many times that I seriously considered ending my life."

Born with major congenital deformities of his right arm and both of his legs, Rajesh had multiple surgeries and had to learn to walk with prosthetics. He was raised by a loving family but says, "There were so many times that I just dreaded going to school. I dreaded the whispers, dreaded trying to keep up with everyone."

In his mid-twenties, however, Rajesh chose to join a friend at a prayer session, and it became a life-altering experience. After battling through depression and feeling so worthless, Rajesh said he realized in a matter of moments—not just cognitively but on an emotional "gut" level—that he could finally take ownership of his life if he could see it as part of a bigger picture and through the eyes of a higher power. He had to let go of the people in his life who were only filling the void. He had to stop fearing his limitations and start focusing on his strengths. The epiphany made him feel free for the first time ever; there was no more embarrassment, just pure opportunity to challenge himself to be his best.

And the harder the challenge the better. Physically and mentally, he wanted to test his faith and commitment to prove to himself, to his family, and to God that his life had forever changed. "I began to focus on trying to make the impossible possible," says Rajesh. "That allowed me to put myself into a future." People didn't think he could run, so Rajesh constructed his own prosthetics and started running. People didn't think he could swim or bike either, but Rajesh customized prosthetics so he could do both. He struggled through short triathlons but improved so dramatically that within a few years, he won a lottery position for the Ironman World Championship triathlon in Kona, Hawaii, in 2010. He became the first—and still only—triple amputee to cross the finish line of this grueling race.

That is where I met Rajesh. I was competing in the Ironman that year as well, and after swimming 2.4 miles in the open ocean and biking 112 miles in sweltering heat, I was at mile 19 of the marathon. It was pitch black as I jogged through the lava fields outside of Kona, and the glow stick I held illuminated only a few feet of the asphalt in front of me. Alone, exhausted, dehydrated, and in terrible pain, I slowed to a hobbled walk and resigned myself to failure; I couldn't possibly finish the final six miles before the midnight deadline.

Then I heard a "click-click, click-click" sound behind me, and it grew louder. Suddenly, I felt a hand on my shoulder, and a kind voice said, "You've come so far, 227; you can't quit now. Just follow me." He'd referred to me only by the number on my bib and didn't tell me his name, but as he passed in front of me, the lights from an oncoming car revealed his silhouette. He had no arm below his right elbow, and the clicking noises were coming from his two prosthetic legs. What an image! What a magnificent moment! His presence had an instant impact on me, and my sense of determination returned. I began to jog—slowly—and then worked to keep pace with him, focusing on nothing but the "click-click" of his legs. My emotions and pain were suppressed, and I managed to finish what I thought was an impossible race.

While I didn't think I'd see this man again, I happened to spot him in the restaurant where I had breakfast the following day. I approached his table and told him that he was the reason I was able to finish the race. Rajesh and I have remained friends ever since, and I'm just one of countless people he's inspired with his story and his actions. He follows a rigorous training schedule to prepare for triathlons and other elite competitions, always practicing what he preaches: "No excuses." Instead of dreading the whispers and stares from others, he's now happy to greet those who see him out training and has brought countless people to tears when he shares his story. He also travels extensively as a motivational speaker, visiting schools, orphanages, and corporate events with the same message of embracing faith in God, overcoming adversity, and maintaining conviction.

IF RAJESH HAD BEEN ASKED to draw a square to represent the four sides of his life when he was a young adult, he would have struggled mightily. He wasn't taking care of his health, he wasn't performing at his best mentally, he held back from forming meaningful

"I smile because I love life. It took me so long to accept and love the life that I have, so now that I'm at peace with myself, I find myself smiling all the time."

— Rajesh Durbal

relationships, and he felt insignificant because he had no sense of his greater purpose. For him, lengthening and strengthening the spiritual side of his life became the starting point that allowed him to improve the other three sides.

While Rajesh struggled to deal with a physical disability, Dan Harris, co-anchor of *Nightline* and the weekend edition of *Good Morning America*, struggled with anxiety. After throwing himself into the life of a workaholic, he began using drugs—first prescription medications and then cocaine—to self-medicate and later had a full-blown panic attack on live national television. Just as Rajesh learned to quiet the voice that told him he wasn't good enough, Dan had to confront his insecurities and calm his "monkey mind," the incessant voices in his head that had propelled him through the ranks of a hypercompetitive profession—to the exclusion of all other sides of his square. In his insightful book *10% Happier*, he chronicles his discovery of meditation and Buddhism.

The book details how mindfulness—actively living in each moment—enabled Dan to slow down and pay attention, and to observe his thoughts without judging them as "right" or "wrong." Through effort and consistent practice, Dan was able to recognize feelings when they arose, such as a particular emotion or the pain of a headache, without becoming overly distressed. This led to incredible mental freedom and creativity in his work, his marriage, and all aspects of his life. While he was once a complete skeptic who thought meditation was a domain reserved for bearded swamis and carefree hippies, he came to realize that the simple habits of meditation could train his mind and make him feel calmer and noticeably happier.

Rajesh was the first—and remains the only—triple amputee to complete the Ironman World Championship triathlon in Kona, Hawaii, in both 2010 and 2011. In addition to training as an elite athlete, he stays busy running his Live Free Foundation, has produced a documentary, and has developed a prosthetic with multipurpose components to improve comfort and remove limitations for other amputees.

Just as exercise benefits us in multiple ways—physically, mentally, and emotionally—recent studies make it clear that spirituality, in its many forms, also improves these three areas. Physically, habits that encourage us to maintain focus, express our gratitude, and find a greater sense of connection result in reduced stress and lower blood pressure and heart rates. This, in turn, alters the expression of our genes through epigenetic pathways and reduces the risk of excessive inflammation that leads to health problems. In terms of mental focus, meditation can improve executive functioning and visuo-spatial processing, and increase control over something called the alpha rhythm—the type of brain wave recorded when we are relaxed. People who can stay calm are able to use this powerful alpha rhythm to screen out distractions and focus on important information, allowing them to solve problems with greater clarity and ease. And emotionally, those who practice meditation have been shown to have more awareness of their feelings and to demonstrate more empathy because of reduced anxiety.

Compared with a control group, adults who had participated in a meditation program for only eight weeks showed more new brain cells (neurogenesis), along with more brain-cell density and connectivity in the hippocampus, the region of the brain associated with memory, emotions, and learning. The study's leader, psychiatrist Dr. Britta Hölzel, said, "It is fascinating to see the brain's plasticity and that, by practicing, we can play an active role in changing the brain and can increase our well-being and quality of life."[6]

Any improvement to our mental functioning has natural, positive ramifications for our lives. Whether it's praying the Rosary, repeating a particular mantra, focusing on our breathing, memorizing the Torah, or finding ways to serve our communities, thinking in a spiritual way modulates existing brain circuits and creates new ones. In short, we can affect the healthy structure of our brains with our own positive thoughts.

Being physically healthier and rediscovering the importance of a spiritual life allowed me to return to Pittsburgh with a clearer sense of *why* than ever before. And as the next two chapters reveal, my improved health and sense of purpose allowed me to address the other two sides of my square: my work life and my relationships. ❑

Exploring the spiritual element of our lives is an incredibly personal and demanding task, and busy lives mean we often struggle to find time for the necessary introspection. On the next few pages, I offer approaches to get you thinking about lengthening and strengthening this side of your square, along with specific ways to take action.

Build a résumé—for your eulogy

In *New York Times* columnist David Brooks' book *The Road to Character*, he explores the big differences between what he calls "résumé virtues" and "eulogy virtues." The former are the skills we list on a page and present to potential employers, while the latter are qualities presented by others at our funerals, descriptions that summarize how we lived our lives.

It's ironic that the Latin *curriculum vitae* translates literally to "course of life," yet our CVs typically represent only what we've learned through education to prepare us for the job market. "We live in a culture that encourages us to think about how to have a great career," writes Brooks, "but leaves many of us inarticulate about how to cultivate the inner life.... We live in a culture that teaches us to promote and advertise ourselves and to master the skills required for success, but that gives little encouragement to humility, sympathy, and honest self-confrontation, which are necessary for building character."[7]

To strengthen your spiritual side, take time to seriously consider the character traits you could include on a résumé for your eulogy. It may help to write down specific good habits that reflect your character: "I try never to be late when I'm meeting people, which makes me considerate," or "I go out of my way to offer sincere compliments to others, which is a form of compassion." This exercise will highlight your strengths and make you aware of issues that could lengthen the spiritual side of your square.

77

Move from the inside out

Countless studies have proven the benefits of spending more time outdoors. Our bodies get important vitamin D from sunlight, and we tend to be more active when we're outside, which counteracts our more sedentary indoor lives. And spending time in nature can also strengthen the spiritual side of our squares. Nature allows us to separate from anything man-made and feed our more primal needs, and the natural world leads to awe, whether it's a stunning vista from a hilltop or the pleasing sensation of holding a smooth pebble in our hand.

- Schedule time each weekend, and several times throughout the week, to spend time outdoors.

- Plan active vacations that get you out into nature.

- Strengthen both your spiritual side and your relationship side by organizing an outdoor activity with friends rather than meeting at a restaurant, movie theater, or mall.

- Learn more about nature by observing and paying attention. Recognizing how plants and animals coexist and understanding nature's cycles teach us lessons in harmony and respect.

- Find a safe place outdoors to exercise, whether it's running, biking, skiing, rowing, or another activity. We tend to enjoy exercise more when we feel the freedom and accomplishment of actually moving as opposed to using treadmills or indoor tracks. And if we enjoy exercising, we'll be much more likely to continue.

- Learn to value the mess as well as the beauty of nature. It's great to take a walk in the rain, get cold out in the snow, or get dirt on your clothes. It wakes us up to the beauties and realities of the world and teaches us lessons about accepting imperfections.

Offer gratitude

We are biologically wired to pay attention to things that may harm us; it's part of our survival instinct. But today we are bombarded by irrelevant or inconsequential negative messages, and when we allow ourselves to be distracted by them, we lose our focus on what we do have.

- Start a gratitude journal, making one entry each morning or each evening. Rather than making general statements like, "I'm grateful for my family," get specific: "I loved the conversation we all had after dinner this evening, especially hearing Grace talk about how much she likes her English class."

- Keep a gratitude jar. Write short "thank yous" on slips of paper and drop them in a jar to be reviewed at the end of the week, or on an occasion like an anniversary or New Year's Eve.

- Make it a goal to thank one person each day for a kindness; just keep it simple and direct. "It meant so much to me that you complimented my work in the staff meeting this morning," or "Thank you again for bringing over that meal when my father was in the hospital last week; it helped us more than you can know."

79

" Thankfulness is a soil in which pride does not easily grow."

— Anglican bishop Michael Ramsey (1904 – 1988)

Be mindful

Our society is a perfect storm for monkey mind because those who multitask usually consider it a point of pride, and ever-present technology creates a constant stream of information, most of which distracts us from the present. Mindfulness is certainly not a new concept—it's the antithesis of monkey mind in the Buddhist tradition—but is now needed more than ever.

- Don't eat mindlessly. Instead, think about food before you eat it (Am I hungry or just bored?), pay attention to food as you're eating it (I love this flavor! Am I starting to feel full?), and notice if you've overeaten (I actually don't feel well now. Ick).

"We're so engaged in doing things to achieve purposes of outer value that we forget that the inner value—the rapture that is associated with being alive—is what it is all about."

— Joseph Campbell

- Make it a priority to pay attention to one thing at a time. Turn off technology that rings, dings, or interrupts the activity you're doing, and focus on completing a small chunk of a task before moving on to another. It's okay to stand in line at the grocery store and not read a magazine. It's better to get into bed and not check your phone. To absorb important information, our brains must have times of quiet.

- Turn tasks into stress relievers. Rather than dreading inevitable chores, try to enjoy folding the warm laundry. Feel the soapy water on your hands as you do dishes. Think of cleaning as taking care of the items in your home, and clear out any items that are cluttering up your home (and, by extension, your thinking).

- Notice things. At least once a day, look at the clouds. Appreciate the sound of laughter in the coffee shop as it mingles with the whoosh of the cappuccino maker. Feel the warmth and smoothness of your child's small hand in yours as you walk together. Actually stop and smell the flowers.

Practice meditation

Many people are skeptical about meditation, dismissing the entire notion because it sounds too new-agey. But this ancient practice has been proven to reduce stress and heighten enjoyment by quieting the internal voice and "background noise" in our heads. Meditation also helps us become more present to everyday situations, training the brain to recognize things as they are instead of immediately attaching judgment or expectations to them. In *10% Happier*, television correspondent Dan Harris says that through meditation, he was able to stop self-medicating with drugs, decrease his anxiety, enjoy his job more, and improve his relationships. It led to an entirely new outlook for Harris, who says that through meditation, "you train yourself to have compassion rather than aversion as your 'default setting.'"[8]

Basic mindfulness meditation requires you to do just three things. First, find a comfortable position—either standing, sitting, or lying down—and make sure that your spine is straight and your chest is open. Next, breathe deeply and focus on the air in your nose or in your chest. Then, whenever your mind wanders, *which it will do over and over again*, gently guide it back to focus on your breaths. ("I cannot stress strongly enough," writes Harris, "that forgiving yourself and starting over is the whole game.")[9] At first, set a timer for just one minute, with the goal of reaching five to ten minutes at a sitting. Consistency is much more important than duration, and the practice will get easier and more relaxing with time.

81

Monkey mind is a Buddhist term meaning "unsettled, restless, inconstant, or confused." Just as a monkey jumps from tree to tree, our minds switch from thought to thought, leaving us distracted and disorganized.

Brain: The Work Side

You are alert. You recognize the danger
as well as the disgrace of a half-used mind.
You are going to gear up your mind to capacity
and share its strength with others.

— William H. Danforth

After experiencing an epiphany about how unbalanced my life had become, the first steps I took to change my circumstances were in a pair of old running shoes. And it soon became obvious that taking responsibility for my physical health allowed me to regain my mental health. During that time, I also reconnected to my religious roots, getting brutally honest with myself about how far I'd veered from core values like respect, compassion, and awe. My square was still far from perfect, but at least two sides—which I'd neglected for so long—had become longer and stronger.

I'd arrived in Bridgeport, Ohio, in mid-January, and by the following December, I was weighing my options about a full return to work. One choice was to stay in the area and open up a solo practice in a community hospital, giving me an opportunity to reestablish myself as a surgeon. My other option was to return to one of the large Pittsburgh hospitals, where I would have a greater opportunity to impact my field but would also face greater pressure and risk falling into my old, unbalanced routines. How did I make the decision? In a single conversation with my mother, she laid it on the line. She first assured me she was strong enough physically and financially for me to leave, and then she said if

I turned away from bigger professional challenges, I would ultimately regret my decision. I knew in my heart she was right.

So I headed back to the same city from which I'd fled one year earlier, wanting to get back to work but also extremely apprehensive. My medical experience in Wheeling had been limited—no conferences, no groundbreaking operations, no keeping up with the latest technologies—so I was left feeling timid in teaching conferences and anxious during operations. My life experience over that previous year, however, had transformed me, and with time, I was able to reestablish myself in my field. Soon, I could sense that I wasn't just returning to my former levels as a surgeon but was rising above. In fact, this period marked some of the most creative and productive work of my career. Why? I was running and exercising regularly now, so all the good stuff that was explained in chapter 5—lower cortisol levels, greater output of good hormones, better sleep and stress management—helped increase my productivity. I also felt a renewed sense of purpose and was conscious of the exciting life I could lead, spiritually recognizing my role in the context of a greater good. And as I will detail in the upcoming chapter, I was also connecting better to colleagues—seeking their collaboration rather than feeling constant competition—and I saw my patients as people to help, rather than just cases to fix.

It was during this time that I also began reading voraciously, not only about the latest developments in my profession, but with the express purpose of broadening my understanding of subjects I'd never taken the time to study. One of the most profound pieces I came across was the ancient Greek myth of Icarus, a young man who'd been imprisoned in a tower on the island of Crete along with his father, the renowned inventor Daedalus. Desperate for an escape, Daedalus fashioned large wings—one pair for himself and another for his son—with the plan of flying to their freedom. Before their bold leap from the tower's window, Daedalus warned Icarus not to fly too low because the spray from the ocean would weigh down the feathers. He also instructed the boy not to fly too high lest the sun's heat melt the wax holding the wings together. In short, he implored Icarus to seek moderation and fly a middle course. Tragically, the boy's eagerness and arrogance pushed him to soar

Daedalus warned Icarus not to fly too low because the spray from the ocean would weigh down the feathers. He also instructed the boy not to fly too high lest the sun's heat melt the wax holding the wings together. In short, he implored Icarus to seek moderation and fly a middle course.

dangerously high, and when his feathers came unglued, Icarus plummeted to his death in what is now called the Icarian Sea.

Having more distance from my own situation, I could see how my inflated ego and desire to impress—what the Greeks called hubris—had always kept me out of balance. In my professional life, I was either soaring arrogantly with my successes or feeling utterly crushed by setbacks and failures. And since my professional life was essentially my *whole* life, I was at its mercy on every peak and in every valley. If I could find a way to ground myself with good physical health, a sense of purpose and humility, and more cooperation with others, my profession would not constantly tempt me to soar or cause me to sink. Aristotle had stressed this "middle between extremes" notion, which is the philosophical Golden Mean echoed in many other spiritual practices. And Icarus' story struck me as another version of Danforth's square—both simple, timeless metaphors that teach the most important lesson in life: find your balance.

In 1986, six years after my return to Pittsburgh, I received the immense honor of being elected president of the Congress of Neurological Surgeons, the largest organization of its kind in North America. When I learned I had to give a presidential address to over 2,000 colleagues, I called Bruce Sorenson, one of the group's past presidents, for advice. "You can talk about whatever you want," I remember him saying, "because the topic doesn't really matter. But whatever you talk about, be sure it comes from the heart." While I would have preferred to offer up a safe little pep talk on the importance of our profession, highlighted with a few facts on the latest neurological research, I knew Bruce was right. Here was my chance to truly reflect on my life-changing experience and then put it out there in a public way, with the possibility that the personal adversity I faced when squaring up my life could serve as an inspiration to others.

I began my speech with the story of Icarus and then spoke honestly about my bizarre journey from neurosurgeon to truck-stop attendant, and how rebalancing my life was the only way to find my way back again. I explained William H. Danforth's square, praising him for his skills as a businessman but praising him even more for his incredible determination to remain a secure, whole person who truly enjoyed the life he'd created. I felt an undeniable connection to the other physicians in the audience, many of whom were overwhelmed, unhealthy, and hurting because they, too, were clinging to the single line of their professions rather than embracing lives fleshed out into stable squares. I received countless comments from colleagues following that speech, and I was deeply honored to be able to inspire them. The experience in turn allowed me to finally re-envision the adversities I'd faced; they hadn't been meaningless tragedies, but were critical lessons that led to self-improvement and renewal.

"I have been a member of the Congress since 1954 and your inspirational presidential address stands out as one of the highlights that I have experienced in medicine at any time. We all need the stimulus produced by such an inspirational delivery."

— Thomas E. Scott Jr., MD,
in a personal letter to me, dated October 10, 1986

TODAY, THE PHRASE "I'm so burned out!" is common when teens, colleagues, or friends become fed up with their lives. They may not have gotten enough sleep, or they're feeling stressed—or bored—by something currently going on at school or work. But actual burnout is much more serious, a clinical syndrome people experience when they're exhausted both emotionally and physically, and weighed down by continual, eroding doubts about their competence and purpose. Rather than simply bandying this term about in casual conversation, we must finally take burnout seriously and recognize it as a real threat to our minds, our bodies, and our job performance.

The cruelest irony is that the industry with some of the most physically and mentally unhealthy professionals is the health care industry itself. While it has traditionally been a high-pressure choice of careers, ongoing turmoil in the American health care industry has placed even more stress on today's doctors. When the Mayo Clinic surveyed 6,880 physicians in 2011, 45 percent of them met the criteria for burnout. When the same physicians were surveyed three years later, 54 percent of them met the criteria. And in response to the statement, "My work schedule leaves me enough time for my personal and/or family life," 37.1 percent of the physicians disagreed or strongly disagreed in 2011, and 44.5 percent responded negatively three years later. When these questions were posed to samples of the general working population of the United States, results showed minimal change in burnout symptoms within the same span of time.[1] A separate study conducted with members of the American College of Surgeons determined that 30 percent of respondents screened positive for depression, and that physician burnout included cynicism, irritability, detachment, and an "over-identification with work to the exclusion of other activities."[2] And the most alarming fact of all? An estimated 400 American doctors kill themselves each year after struggling with issues like depression, anxiety, or addiction.[3]

Herbert Freudenberger, a German-born American psychologist and Fellow of the American Psychological Association, first used the term "burnout" in 1974 and published a book that became the standard reference for the condition. Since then, numerous studies have shown that burnout rates are indeed higher for those who work in the helping professions, including health care, teaching, social work, and counseling. These are the jobs most difficult to see as "just jobs" because they deal so constantly and directly with human emotion, human potential, and in the worst cases, suffering and loss of life. In a piece reprinted in the *Washington Post* in 2014, professional-turned-teacher Ellie Herman described how she lasted five years in the Los Angeles school district before burning out and leaving her position. "Everything felt like an emergency," she wrote. "And there was never enough time.... Neuroscientists have identified a condition they call executive function overload, during which your brain, overstimulated from continual crisis management, becomes unable to think clearly or feel emotions. I can see now that this happened to me."[4]

Those in the helping professions certainly haven't cornered the market on job burnout, however. Falling prey to this kind of overload can happen to people in any field when they feel as if they have no control over their work environment, are stuck in dysfunctional dynamics or have unclear job expectations, or if there's a significant mismatch between their personal values and the values held by their employer. Another large factor in burnout is the type of activity required for a job. Positions with constant deadlines and intense intellectual work can be taxing, especially when work hours routinely spill into personal time. Burnout can occur on the other extreme as well—when jobs are mundane and monotonous, for instance, or when a business is struggling and too little activity threatens employment.

SO WHAT CAN BE DONE to address the very real problem of job burnout? I can take a first step by making an obvious statement, but it's something many people don't take enough time to consider: your skills should match the requirements of your job, and you should actually want to do the job you're doing. In his bestselling book *The Element*, British education and creativity expert Ken Robinson laments that too many people don't have a true picture of their own capabilities, frequently because of mediocre educational experiences that don't allow them to discover, celebrate, or pursue their true talents. And without an awareness of what intrinsically motivates them, they often cannot find what Robinson calls the Element—the work that truly connects them to their purpose. In addition, adults often

Too many people don't have a true picture of their own capabilities, frequently because of mediocre educational experiences that don't allow them to discover, celebrate, or pursue their true talents. These limitations clearly pain Ken Robinson, who rejoices in the incredible diversity of human potential.

make the mistake of thinking that they're stuck with work they don't enjoy because they assume life can only be lived linearly. "Many people have not found their Element because they don't understand their constant potential for renewal," explains Robinson. "This limited view of our own capacities can be compounded by our peer groups, by our culture, and by our own expectations of ourselves."[5]

These limitations clearly pain Robinson, who rejoices in the incredible diversity of human potential. Much like Simon Sinek's message of concentric circles with the ever-important *why* in the middle, Robinson's notion of the Element is based on having the self-awareness of your true skill set and what intrinsically motivates you; knowing what you're good at and actually doing that. Such awareness and commitment, he writes, "is essential to your well-being and ultimate success, and, by implication, to the health of our organizations and the effectiveness of our educational systems."[6]

A second step toward preventing job burnout has nothing to do with our jobs; instead it looks at how we're actually living the rest of our lives. Constant references to the notion of work/life balance makes it sound like a cliché, but consider that expert advice on finding a healthy equilibrium between our jobs and our personal lives falls into three basic categories:

(1) the importance of getting physical exercise and adequate sleep, (2) the value of finding joy in meaningful relationships, and (3) the benefits of spending time in introspection and seeing ourselves in some greater context. These are not fads, shortcuts, or quick fixes—they are, in fact, *the other three sides of Danforth's square.* When our work becomes the only thing that defines us, even when we enjoy our jobs and have talents to contribute, our lives lose a sense of greater purpose. When we are able to flesh out our squares to keep ourselves healthy, connected, and grounded, however, we're able to live as our greatest, truest selves.

I CONSCIOUSLY BEGAN to reconstruct my square by focusing first on the physical side, and Rajesh Durbal found his way to a purposeful and balanced life by discovering the importance of faith. And when Dr. Elizabeth Tyler-Kabara found herself out of shape and "always, always in crisis mode," she was able to establish more balance in her life by rethinking the boundaries of her important work.[7]

Elizabeth earned her bachelor's degree at Duke University, where she double-majored in biomedical and electrical engineering. She then went to work at the National Institutes of Health (NIH) before moving on to earn both an MD and a PhD from Vanderbilt University by 1997. Following over a dozen years of moving to different cities for medical school,

"I wanted this beautiful daughter and this great husband, and I wanted this amazing career in neurosurgery that I'd worked so hard for—it was important work to help other people. But I was really unhealthy. Craziness, busyness had just become normal, and I'd lost control somewhere along the line."

— Dr. Elizabeth Tyler-Kabara

residencies, and internships, she finally settled in Pittsburgh. She'd met the man who would become her husband while working at NIH, and while they were an extremely compatible couple, she realized she rarely made the time to stay connected to friends. Then, after gaining excessive weight with a very difficult pregnancy, she found herself physically out of shape for the first time in her life. To complicate matters even more, soon after delivering a daughter, Elizabeth was given a title that put her in charge of a large administrative, clinical, and research staff, and she was overwhelmed with responsibilities.

"I wanted this beautiful daughter and this great husband," explained Elizabeth, "and I wanted this amazing career in neurosurgery that I'd worked so hard for—it was important work to help other people. But I was really unhealthy. When I saw myself in a photo I hardly recognized my own face, a double chin…" Her voice trailed off and she shook her head. "Craziness, busyness had just become normal, and I'd lost control somewhere along the line."

Elizabeth didn't quit her job or even cut back her hours. Instead, she accepted the hectic, unpredictable, exciting aspects of her profession. She chose to "lean in" to her work—a nod to Facebook COO Sheryl Sandberg's concept of the importance of women embracing their role in the workplace—while making a series of small but critical changes in her life. She started keeping track of what she was eating using a simple online program, which led to eliminating things like soda, white bread, and mindless snacking. She also established regular dinners at home with her husband and daughter, and made it a priority to get active as a family—biking, hiking, skiing—anything to be out in nature and be together.

Although Elizabeth knew nothing about William Danforth's concept of the square during this time, she was intuitively making changes that lengthened and strengthened the three sides of her life unrelated to her work. After I explained Danforth's square to her, Elizabeth thought for a moment and pointed out that she often combines two or three of the sides into one activity. Biking, for example, allows her to stay physically fit, spend time with her family, and be out in nature, which has always nurtured her spiritually. "I've been multitasking in order to be efficient with my time, haven't I?" she laughed. "But look at that. It works!"

91

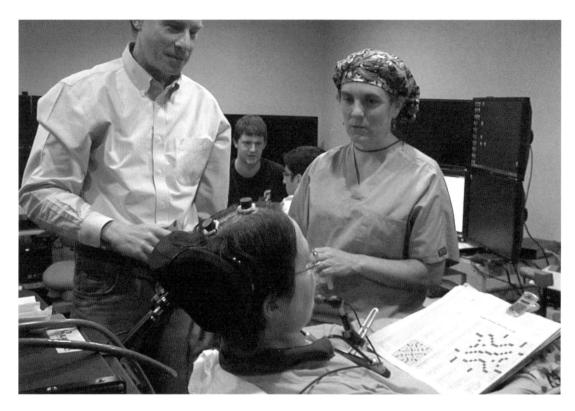

92

Elizabeth is joined by fellow researcher Dr. Andrew Schwartz and two assistants at a facility at the University of Pittsburgh Medical Center. Their test subject, Jan Scheuermann, is a quadriplegic who learned to control a robotic arm with her thoughts using a revolutionary brain-computer interface. At right is Elizabeth with her husband and their young daughter on vacation together.

Elizabeth has found great success in her career, but she also savors the many other ways she has found success in her life. When I complimented her on all the incredible work she has done, Elizabeth smiled and said, "Thank you. Really. Even when it's crazy around the hospital, people tell me, 'You're entirely too happy.' But choosing to be miserable really just doesn't add anything to my day."

Elizabeth made time to have a full life outside of her career and also remains truly passionate about the work she does. Currently an associate professor at the University of Pittsburgh's School of Medicine, Elizabeth has also been a leading researcher on mind-controlled robotic prosthetics for people with paralysis. After making great strides with a male subject in 2011, Elizabeth and her team conducted an extensive study several years later with Jan, a 53-year-old woman with quadriplegia. First, Elizabeth implanted two small electrode grids in the region of Jan's brain that would normally control the right arm and hand. These electrodes were then hooked up to a computer so the team could monitor Jan's brain cell activity when she thought about moving her own right hand. With practice, Jan was able to move a robotic arm with her own thoughts, and her proudest moment came when she used the robotic arm to bring a chocolate bar to her lips and take a bite; she hadn't been able to feed herself in nearly 15 years. In 2016, Elizabeth and her team worked with another paralyzed subject, this time testing how to send sensory and motor signals from the robotic hand back to the subject's brain so he could essentially "feel" through the device.

While considerably more work needs to be done to make mind-controlled robotics feasible for everyday use, what Elizabeth and her team are doing has the potential to revolutionize the lives of vets, children, and adults who face the daily fears and frustrations of paralysis. This powerful work motivates Elizabeth, as does her specialty as a pediatric neurosurgeon. "I'm in the position to help families who are typically overwhelmed with their situations," she explains. "Being able to sit down with these anxious parents, to spend time with them and explain what we can do to help the child they love so dearly, is one of the most spiritual things I do."

Elizabeth and her colleagues mark their milestones with interviews and published papers, of course. But when they're able to improve the lives of their pediatric patients through successful surgeries, they also throw big parties with the families, giving Elizabeth another chance to find balance: her husband and daughter are an integral part of the celebrations. Elizabeth has found great success in her career, but she also savors the many other ways she has found success in her life. When I complimented her on all the incredible work she has done, Elizabeth smiled and said, "Thank you. Really. Even when it's crazy around the hospital, people tell me, 'You're entirely too happy.' But choosing to be miserable really just doesn't add anything to my day."

94   WORK HAD BEEN THE LONGEST—and in all honesty, essentially the only—side of my square for a great deal of my life. I put everything into my career, all because of my incredibly narrow definition of success and a foolish assumption that professional achievement was all that mattered. Regrets flooded in, however, when I realized I'd allowed all the other important pieces of my life to simply fall by the wayside. And some of the most important pieces? People—the final side of the square to be explored. ◻

"Achieve greatly through a clear and powerful urge to accomplish something notable; through a superior persistence; through marked faith in yourself...high enthusiasm, intellectual curiosity—the itch to understand."

— William H. Danforth

While the other "Think & Act" sections are designed to help you lengthen and strengthen that side of the square, this section is a little different. For many people, lengthening their work sides is not the issue; too many hours at work is the very thing that caused imbalance in their lives. This section looks instead at prioritizing tasks, working smarter rather than harder, and making relationships at work more meaningful so your job can be more fulfilling.

Make a list

When facing frustrations with your job, try making a two-column list.

- In the first column, write down specific things that you enjoy about your job.
- In the second, try to pinpoint what isn't working.

This very basic exercise will help you identify the elements of your job that you can celebrate, which can be hugely beneficial if it helps you find ways of going after more of the good stuff in the first column. Did you enjoy the experience of training new employees? Have you mastered a new computer program that would allow you to work on projects you'd enjoy?

95

Next, see what you can do about the second column. Do you hate the commute? Perhaps you'd consider a move, or could ask about working a day or two from home. Pay too low? Feeling overwhelmed by the workload? Unhappy with your team? Propose specific solutions to these problems to see if you can exert some control over the situation.

If your first column is practically empty and your second column warrants a second piece of paper, it may be time to consider a job change. *But be sure the items in the second column actually have to do with the specifics of your job and aren't areas that could be addressed if you focused on strengthening the other three sides of your square.* (Now go back and reread that last sentence several times so that it really sinks in.)

Find your why

Simon Sinek proposed his model of three concentric circles—the outer listing *what*, the middle stating *how*, and the center asking *why*—as a way to help companies identify or reevaluate their values and goals. I propose a similar exercise for individuals who are considering (or reconsidering) their own careers. It may also help to combine Sinek's *why* with the concept of "crystallizing experiences," developed by David Feldman of Tufts University and later by Howard Gardner of Harvard. These are occasions when an object or encounter piques a person's interest so much that it has a profound influence on his or her future passions.

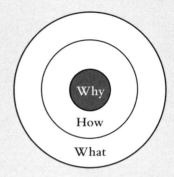

Albert Einstein's father, for example, gave him a compass when he was barely five years old. The boy was so intrigued by it that it became his favorite possession and sparked his great interest in the beautiful mysteries of science. For me, a crystallizing experience happened during my senior year in med school. While rounding with a chief resident of neurosurgery, I watched as he examined a patient who was experiencing headaches and blurred vision. The resident asked the patient to focus on a point in front of him, then wiggled his own fingers on either side of the patient's head. When it was clear the patient had no peripheral vision, the resident made a diagnosis of a pituitary tumor at the base of his skull that was compressing his optic nerves. I was so amazed by this simple 30-second test—based entirely on the doctor's understanding of the workings of neuroanatomy and the surgical curing of blindness—that I chose neurosurgery and have never second-guessed my decision!

Watch Simon Sinek's TED Talk and then draw your own set of concentric circles. Try to describe what you do, how you do it, and then consider why you do it. Do you have a clear *why*? Does it connect to any crystallizing experience you've had in your life?

When exploring all of this, consider a quote attributed to Sinek: "Working hard for something we don't care about is called stress; working hard for something we love is called passion."

Work smarter, not harder

This may sound like a trite suggestion, but research proves there are real benefits to working more efficiently in less time. The best ways to go about it?

Always start the day with a clear agenda of what must get done, and tackle these items as soon as possible.

• Break a large task down into small chunks, keeping track of what's been accomplished.

• Make sure you (or the members of your team) are working on a clearly defined task that is well communicated to everyone. Nothing is more inefficient than taking the time to solve the wrong problem.

• Take regular breaks throughout the day, which allows your brain to process information and stay alert. A break outdoors will reap even more restorative benefits.

• Minimize the work you must do outside of regular hours, because that's the time to focus on the other sides of the square—including hobbies, eating well, exercising, getting enough sleep, and enjoying time with friends and family.

Strengthen your relationships at work

Forming healthy work relationships gets tricky if the environment is overly competitive. But when collaboration can trump competitiveness, both the business and its employees will benefit.

• Be willing to open up to colleagues so they get to know you as a person. When workers interact socially to build up camaraderie, it can change the entire culture of the workplace.

• Offer compliments and speak positively about others whenever possible, especially to a co-worker's superiors. This builds trust and confidence in those around you.

• Listen twice as much as you talk. It makes other people feel as though they truly matter, and you learn a great deal in the process.

• Do everything you can to demonstrate good manners: maintain eye contact, give a firm handshake, offer sincere thanks, don't gossip, and speak using proper grammar. These all go a long way toward your reputation and ultimately your own satisfaction with a job.

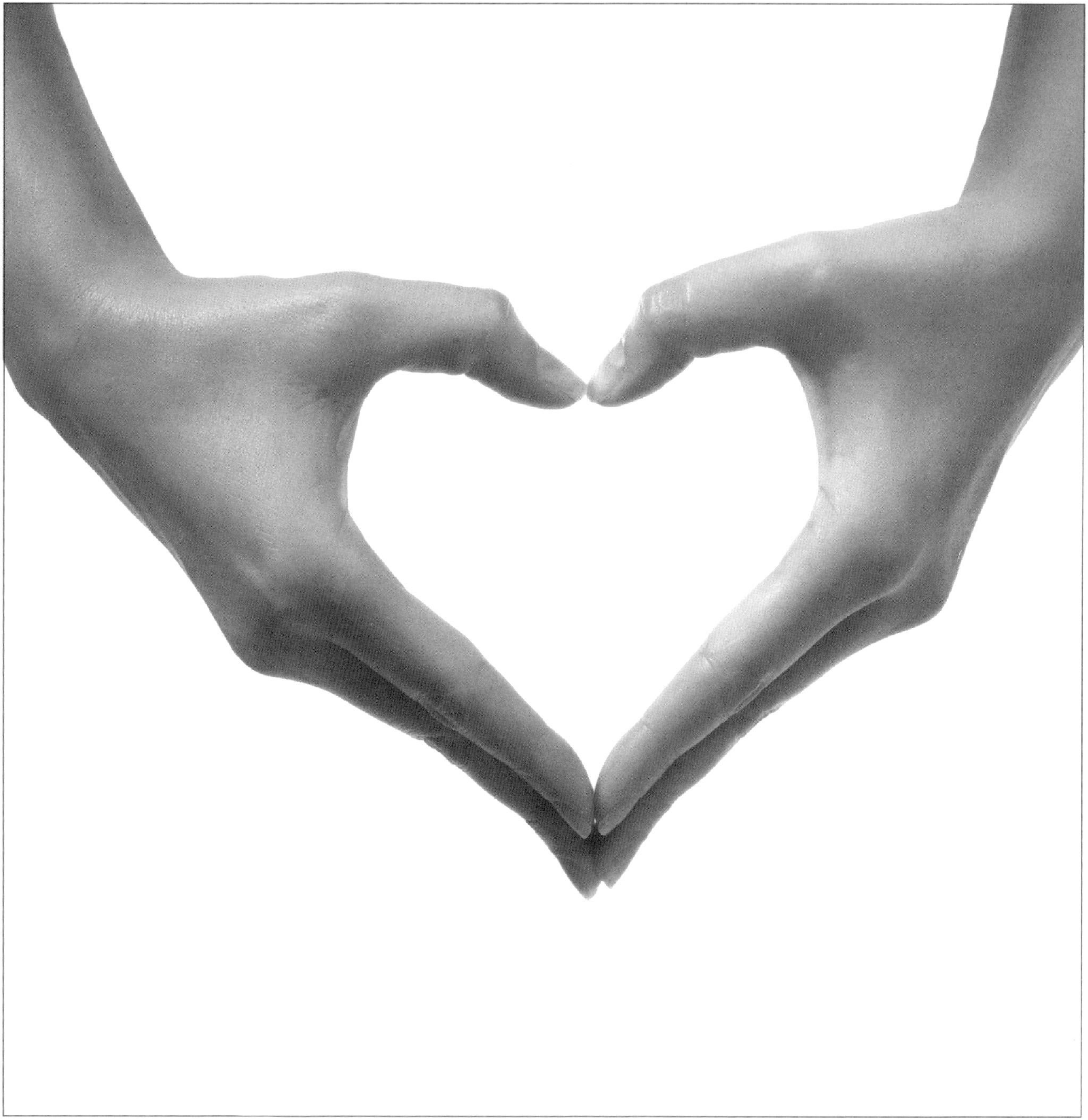

Heart: The Relationship Side

I dare you to develop the fine art of finding,
making, and keeping friends by
genuine giving of your time and personality
to others. Look for the best in people.

— William H. Danforth

AT THE SAME TIME that I was making my decision to leave Bridgeport and return to a job in Pittsburgh, I had also begun to fully address my failing marriage. My mind had become less foggy after my depression lifted, and I'd been trying to build a better moral foundation by revisiting my religious roots. When I faced the hard realities of the situation, I realized I could finally find relief—for my wife and for myself—by being brutally honest about my role in the relationship. While we ultimately ended up divorcing, we did find ways to rekindle some kindness and were able to support one another through the difficult process. And I'm grateful that our amiable relationship has continued for over 30 years.

One thing that became obvious to me while living in West Virginia with my mother (and yes, I know Sigmund Freud would have had a field day with that situation) was how the expectations I had for my own marriage were affected by my parents' marriage. Theirs had been the stereotypical Old World relationship common to so many immigrants: the woman as subservient and the man as the headstrong patriarch. I married an intelligent, kind, and capable woman but carried this outdated notion of roles along with me, and as I described in chapter 2, I felt I'd succeeded on some level just by checking "marriage" off my to-do list. I had very little understanding of what was required to have an ongoing, loving, equal partnership, and even when it became painfully and glaringly obvious that I was making poor choices in my relationship, I ran away from the problems—straight toward my career—rather than turning to face them as I should have.

Psychologist Daniel Goleman published *Emotional Intelligence: Why It Can Matter More Than IQ* in 1995, using groundbreaking science to set forth the idea that how we handle our emotions—in both our professional and personal lives—has significant impact on our health and our happiness. Through countless studies, Goleman found that "academic intelligence has little to do with emotional life" and that "people with high IQs can be stunningly poor pilots of their private lives."[1]

And what an ironic quote for me to include here! I've learned so much in my career as a neurosurgeon, literally touching and healing human brains thousands of times. But the high IQ that helped me get through medical school and residency didn't guarantee me any success in my personal relationships. That element of my square had been precariously short leading up to my crisis, and in full disclosure, it has remained the most difficult side for me to maintain. Why? It was actually through the writing of this book that I came to realize something that now seems all too evident: I can assert significant control over the physical side of my life with the choices I make, and strengthening both the spiritual side and the work side of my square is also very much mine to manage. The relationship side, however, by its very definition, requires me to give up a degree of that control, making me both more vulnerable and more accountable to others. So it has taken repeated (and a few very notable) mistakes on my part to learn the value of emotional intelligence, and how investing fully in relationships is what offers the most important and lasting rewards in our lives.

IN MOST ANCIENT CULTURES, people agreed there were two ways to express a truth. Defined by the Greeks as *logos* and *mythos*, both approaches were considered equally vital and valid. *Logos*, Greek for "word, reason," was the pragmatic, rational mode that led to logical and practical thinking, while *mythos*—"story"—dealt with the intuitive, emotional,

"When a mythical narrative was symbolically re-enacted," says religious historian Karen Armstrong, "it brought to light something 'true' about human life and the way our humanity worked, even if its insights, like those of art, could not be proven rationally."[2] Armstrong also points out that "our scientifically oriented knowledge seeks to master reality, explain it, and bring it under the control of reason, but a delight in the unknowing has also been part of the human experience."[3]

subjective domains. While *logos* could explain a great deal to these ancients, they also learned through *mythos*, which allayed their fears and allowed them to find richer meaning in their lives. The mythological stories they shared taught timeless, valuable lessons even though they were not based on any known science—stories about a mother's love for her child, the dangers of arrogance, or the journeys of great heroes. Journalist Bill Moyers, in a discussion with renowned mythologist Joseph Campbell, asked, "And these myths tell me how others have made the passage, and how I can make the passage?" To which Campbell replied, "Yes, and also what are the beauties of the way."[4]

Over time, however, the results of *logos* thinking came to be considered reliable facts, while what was once considered a truth expressed by *mythos* was altered. At best it was relegated to fiction, but in some cases it was seen as an outright falsity. Indeed, the word "myth" is now commonly used to refer to an unfounded or unverifiable idea. For most of my life, I was strictly a *logos* person, feeling much more comfortable in a classroom, a lab, or a lecture hall. I liked relying on empirical reasoning, and I could master information through study. The critical lesson that Danforth's square taught me, however, is that important truths about the elements of our lives—all four sides—can only be revealed through both *logos* (logical thinking) and *mythos* (meaningful thoughts and emotional experiences).

Physically, for example, science and data help us better understand the workings of our bodies, but the jubilant sensations that come with good health and fluid movement are profoundly real and become our subjective reward. Spiritually, a great deal of religion gets boiled down to creeds, codes, and rote responses, but when the focus shifts back to *mythos* and awe, spiritual practices are elevated from mere dogma to decent, moral actions and positive expressions of kindness. And in terms of the workplace, countless studies have shown that people with careers that allow them to use their strengths and feel a sense of intuitive purpose have the highest job satisfaction.

So what about the fourth side of our square, human relationships? Here is where *logos* and *mythos* are perhaps most strongly linked, because positive interaction with others is built on a foundation of both rational thought and emotional competency. We've struggled throughout our history with the exact geography of *mythos* and *logos*. Aristotle, for instance, thought the heart was the seat of all thinking, and Egyptians typically discarded the enigmatic brain when mummifying a body; the heart, after all, was the organ that moved and made all the noise! Then it became a common notion that we think with our heads and feel with our hearts; love emanated from our chests, and when someone lacked affection, he was said to

102

"If music be the food of love, play on."

This Shakespeare quote shows the Bard knew how closely music connects to emotions. And human relationships, from the highs of love to lows of loss, remain the most popular topic in music. In his sweetly philosophical song "I Forgot That Love Existed," award–winning performer Van Morrison references Plato and Socrates and goes on to sing the lines, "If my heart could do my thinking / and my head begin to feel / I would look upon the world anew / and know what's truly real."

have a cold heart. It's only been a little more than a hundred years since we've determined that all thoughts and feelings originate in the brain—with rational thought located in the prefrontal cortex and emotions seated in our limbic systems.

Healthy relationships, therefore, depend on the control we acquire over the analytical and emotional parts of our brain. The better these two regions of our brains get along, the better we can expect to get along with others. But as explained in the very first chapter of this book, the circuits and connections that allow us to reason are less well developed than those for the evolutionarily older circuits for emotion. Consequently, our emotions can more easily escape conscious control. The same monkey mind that can occur because of multitasking at work—the mind that can rob us of a sense of peace in our daily lives—can also devastate our relationships unless, of course, we can become more mindful.

A LONGITUDINAL STUDY begun in 1990 by psychologist John Gottman confirms a remarkable predictor of marital happiness. In a lab on the campus of the University of Washington, Gottman set up several rooms to look like a comfortable, hotel-like retreat. He brought in a total of 130 newly married couples and had each couple spend one day in this relaxed environment. As a couple interacted—cooking, talking, listening to music—Gottman took note of how the partners made requests for a connection. These "bids," as Gottman called them, included anything that required a response from the spouse, and the spouse could either "turn away" from this request for a connection, or "turn toward" it.

One example Gottman used was when a husband who had a strong interest in birds saw a goldfinch out the window and said to his wife, "Look at that beautiful bird outside!" By choosing to share this information out loud, the husband was asking his partner for acknowledgment and support of his interest; he was making a "bid" for her to connect to him in some way. The wife could choose many ways to respond, from completely ignoring his comment or sighing with annoyance (degrees of "turning away") to asking a follow-up question or actually going to the window to see the bird (a sign of "turning toward").

When Gottman followed up with the same couples six years later, he found that the reactions he'd seen them make to each other's bids had affected their marriages. Couples that had divorced within those six years or who were living in unhappy marriages had demonstrated "turn-toward bids" only 33 percent of the time, while couples that were still happily together had "turn-toward bids" 87 percent of the time. Stunningly, Gottman's initial observations were 94 percent accurate in determining whether couples would be together and happy several years later. "Much of it comes down to the spirit the couples bring to the relationship," writes journalist Emily Esfahani Smith in a piece about Gottman's study for *The Atlantic*. "Do they bring kindness and generosity; or contempt, criticism, and hostility?"[5]

When I read through this article, I was struck by the sheer simplicity and common-sense notion of Gottman's concept of an emotional bid. From personal experience—yes, a total of three marriages and three divorces—I know how busy, ungrounded lives lead to selfish thinking and emotional reservations that mean you're operating a marriage in contempt mode. After conducting frequent studies on marriage, Gottman began categorizing people as either "masters" of relationships or "disasters" of relationships, and I have to say that I identify much more with the latter. Whenever a marriage got difficult, it was easier for me to turn away from my spouse and turn toward my career—a true example of someone married to his job. What I consistently overlooked was how, at their most basic level, relationships are about two people creating a haven of respect and kindness, with both partners recognizing the need for an ongoing, give-and-take mindset. Using all of my hard lessons learned, I am now delighted to be in a loving and stable relationship—11 years and counting!

IN THE THREE PREVIOUS CHAPTERS, I described how I began with my physical life in order to regain my balance, Rajesh Durbal tapped into his spiritual side, and Elizabeth Tyler-Kabara began by reimagining her work life. For someone who has excelled with relationships, I look to my longtime friend, poet and professor emeritus Sam Hazo.

Born in 1928 to Lebanese and Assyrian immigrants, Sam was born and raised in Pittsburgh.[6] He shows obvious delight when he tells the story that his mother had no

"I would have loved to know my mother. For years after she died, people who knew her would tell me such nice things about her; they would say how remarkable she was, and then they'd be in tears. She had that effect on people."

— Sam Hazo

A photo of Sam, above, who enlisted in the United States Marine Corps and served during the Korean War. The group photo shows Sam (left) with his younger brother, Robert, and their maternal aunt Katherine Abdou. She stepped in to raise her nephews after her sister passed away when the boys were very young.

intention of marrying the man her father had chosen for her, but instead married the man she loved. They had two sons, first Sam and then his younger brother, but their love affair ended all too soon; Sam's mother died when he was only five years old. "I would have loved to know my mother," he says. "For years after she died, people who knew her would tell me such nice things about her; they would say how remarkable she was, and then they'd be in tears. She had that effect on people." He takes great solace in knowing how much his mother loved him, however, and he was also loved dearly by his maternal aunt and grandfather, who essentially raised Sam and his brother because Sam's father traveled so extensively for his job.

Shortly after graduating magna cum laude from the University of Notre Dame, Sam joined the United States Marine Corps, serving in the Korean War and completing his tour as a captain. He later earned a master's degree from Duquesne University and a doctorate from the University of Pittsburgh. He took on several teaching posts before joining the faculty in the English Department at Duquesne, where he served as a professor for 43 years. In 1966, he also founded Pittsburgh's renowned International Poetry Forum, which he continued to lead until the organization closed its doors in 2009. The unprecedented forum hosted more than 400 events over the years, bringing in remarkable poets—W. H. Auden, Pulitzer Prize winner Anne Sexton, Nobel Prize winner Seamus Heaney, United States poet laureate Robert Pinsky—along with patrons of the arts like Princess Grace of Monaco, Gregory Peck, Peter Ustinov, Anthony Hopkins, and Eva Marie Saint. Sam was a National Book Award Finalist, and he was chosen by Governor Robert Casey to serve as the first poet laureate of the state of Pennsylvania, a post that he held for over a decade.

Through all of these years, Sam's wife, Mary Anne—whom he married in 1955—was by his side. "It was love at last sight," he says with a smile, adding he always knew he would spend his life with her. "I remember, early on in our relationship, I was talking to her and said, 'After we're married...' And she interrupted me and asked, 'Is there a question in there somewhere?'" Mary Anne was integral to the Poetry Forum's success from its inception, taking part in every element of the organization. Husband and wife also worked together to raise their son, now a musician and composer whose works are performed worldwide. Sam

" From port to port we learn that 'depths last longer than heights,'

that years are meant to disappear like wakes,

that nothing but the sun stands still.

We share the sweeter alphabets of laughter and the slower languages of pain.

Common as coal, we find in one another's eyes

the quiet diamonds that are worth the world.

Drawn by the song of our keel, who are we but horizons coming true?"

An image of Sam and his bride on their wedding day in 1955, and a treasured photo of them still dancing years later. The excerpt is from Sam's poem "To All My Mariners in One."[7] When asked whether these words could represent his ultimate view on the power of relationships, he says, "Yes. It's all that matters, really."

himself has been a son, brother, captain, teacher, husband, father, organizer, writer, poet, and playwright, and he has thrived in these people-centric roles. Yet it is not due to any extroverted, boisterous, commanding personality; in fact, Sam is a thoughtful, introspective man who is simply fascinated by all aspects of the human condition, most notably the stories we can share with one another.

As a professor, Sam tried to expose his students to these great stories and to imbue them with a sense of curiosity and independence. "I think the role of a teacher," he says, "is to lead students into the jungle and then watch as they try and hack their way out. I stressed deep thinking, I stressed the need to accept that we're not perfect, and I always talked about the possibilities that come with revision." All great advice, of course, and not just for English majors. Sam lights up when he talks about the letters he's received from his former students, checking in with him and thanking him for inspiring them in the classroom. And the people Sam met through the International Poetry Forum inspired him as well.

It was these kinds of connections that spurred Sam on and gave him the fodder he needed to write his award-winning poetry. Any connection, as a matter of fact, meant a great deal to him. "At the grocery store, we're usually all about efficiency, aren't we?" he comments. "We have our own list, our own paths. But choosing the longest line and starting up a conversation with the person next to you is always an interesting experiment. It's like suddenly being handed a new book. Learning someone else's story can be such a privilege." Now nearing 90, Sam is still writing poetry about relationships, and his recent collection is titled *And the Time Is: Poems, 1958 – 2013.*

Unfortunately, Mary Anne was diagnosed with dementia shortly after that publication, and Sam had to find ways to help her adjust to her declining faculties. Because so much of their relationship had been based on their ability to communicate well, and on their mutual love for the written and spoken word, it was devastating for Sam to witness Mary Anne struggle with her memory and her ability to speak and read. And in the summer of 2016, Mary Anne passed away at the age of 89, in the same house where she and Sam had raised their son. "Up to the very end, I was able to understand Mary Anne, to communicate with her, by just looking into her eyes," Sam says. "Losing her has been the first truly, truly painful adversity in my life, but I did my very best to take care of her simply because I loved her."

Earlier in this chapter, the main relationship I focused on was marriage. But as Sam Hazo's story so clearly illustrates, we play many different complex relationship roles in our lives. At different points, we may be someone's child, friend, student, colleague, parent, spouse, ex, sibling, boss, teacher, neighbor, mentor...or a dozen other roles. Despite the fact that technology has made our world feel smaller—from video conference calls to an international Internet to countless social media channels—it remains incredibly difficult to maneuver our way through life, coordinating dance steps with all the other people we meet. While I could come up with a long list of social skills that can lengthen and strengthen the relationship side of our squares, I will focus briefly on just two: harmony and empathy.

Harmonia was the Greek goddess of concord and unity, the antithesis of Eris, who spread nothing but discord and strife. Harmony in music is created when two or more pitches are played together to create a pleasing sound, and we say a work of art is harmonious when all of its parts complement one another. In the social sense, groups that work in harmony—from an individual family to an educational institution, a corporation, or an entire country—are inevitably more successful than those that don't.

In *Emotional Intelligence*, Daniel Goleman writes that when any team works together, the tangible skills of each individual clearly contribute to the whole. But how well the team members accomplish any task has less to do with their average intelligence quotients (their IQ) and much more to do with their emotional quotients (their EQ). Citing an experiment by Yale psychologists Robert Sternberg and Wendy Williams, Goleman writes, "The single most important factor in maximizing the excellence of a group's product was the degree to which the members were able to create a state of internal harmony, which lets them take advantage of the full talent of their members."[8]

So if harmony is basically parts making up a whole, it must begin with each of us first being in tune with ourselves. Harkening back to earlier points made in this book, it's important that we find our own sense of purpose, know our Element, exercise, meditate, or

Living in Harmony

Old Economy Village, located just outside Pittsburgh, Pennsylvania, was the third model community set up by the Harmony Society in the early 1800s. Members, known as Harmonites, prospered by working together and sharing communal property, and a statue of a figure they called Harmony still stands in the garden of this historic site. Harmony is also what our bodies seek through the process known as homeostasis. From the Greek *homeo* (same) and *stasis* (still), this is what allows our dynamic systems to cooperate with one another to maintain steady vital states, including consistent body temperatures and dependable oxygen levels in our blood. Taking care of our bodies allows us to maintain this important homeostasis.

do enough yoga so we have the knowledge and wherewithal to actually play our own note correctly. Only then do we have enough self-awareness and emotional intelligence to see our part in context and to show a second critical social skill: empathy.

As any child psychologist can tell you—and most new parents quickly learn—babies are focused on their own requirements and don't show a whole lot of empathy. There really is no reasoning with a hungry newborn or tired toddler; with little knowledge of the wide world around them, their immediate needs take center stage. As a child learns language and begins to read the cues of others, however, their world expands enough for them to understand someone else's perspective, show some empathy, and share a toy. Throughout adolescence, empathy continues to develop, but it's the atypical child who can consistently recognize the needs of others and respond with compassionate, selfless acts. Unfortunately, a lack of empathy may be becoming more typical for adults as well. By definition, self-centeredness and a sense of entitlement negate the ability to demonstrate the kindness required for empathy, and this can lead to everything from disrespect and discrimination to violence and abuse.

And here is where we must seek balance. We want to raise children to speak their minds, to compete, and to advocate for their own rights, but we also need to foster their selflessness. Companies need to hold their employees to consistently high standards, but bosses should also be able to show empathy. The medical profession must adhere to elements of rules-based practices, but doctors should also know the reward of following their intuition and learning to communicate empathetically with their patients. So here we find a parallel to the ancient truths that arise from both *logos* and *mythos*: both are important to help us find meaning in our lives, just as both independence and empathy are keys to fostering healthy relationships. Daniel Pink commits an entire chapter to empathy in his book *A Whole New Mind*, and he notes, "Empathy is neither a deviation from intelligence nor the single route to it. Sometimes we need detachment; many other times we need attunement. And the people who will thrive will be those who can toggle between the two."[9]

I SPENT SO MUCH of my early career chasing success, and I mindlessly filled my days with hassle and hurry. As a result, I've slogged through several terrible, hopeless periods bearing the weight of how those choices affected my personal relationships. I also experienced complete devastation when, after adopting our two children, my first wife gave birth to a son with severe neurological damage and profound cerebral palsy. Then years later, I was emotionally wrecked all over again when our adopted son was killed in a car accident when he was only 21 years old. Through great trial and tribulation, however, I've learned to pay attention to the lessons that experience teaches about the need for strong, reliable, joyful relationships. And I've found harmony within myself so that I can be a better colleague, a more empathetic doctor, and a more sincere friend and companion. Most importantly, I've strived to become a better father and am unspeakably proud of my four grown daughters, all successful and happy in their own ways. I also have a sweet granddaughter and feel very lucky that she lives so close by. It's impossible for me to regret any of the relationships I've had—no matter how painful they may have been in the end—when I see the faces of the beautiful women whom I'm blessed to be able to call my children.

I saved the relationship side of Danforth's square for last because, as I said earlier, it has been the hardest for me to keep in check. While I've been able to commit myself to consistent exercise and a good diet, and I've had little trouble staying focused on professional goals, it has taken me much longer to get in true harmony with myself, to recognize specific, healthy ways to empathize with others, and to then regularly carry these actions out. But I have certainly reaped the benefits and can see now how foolish it was to try to minimize the immense value of this side of my square. In his moving book *Tuesdays With Morrie*, author Mitch Albom meets with his former professor—who is dying from amytrophic lateral sclerosis (ALS)—to discuss life's Big Questions and to capture Morrie's wisdom for posterity. On a day when they are discussing the importance of family and community, Morrie quotes poet W. H. Auden and says, "Love each other or perish." When Mitch asks for more information, Morrie simply responds, "Love each other or perish. It's good, no? And it's so true. Without love, we are birds with broken wings."[10] ◻

Birds of a feather...

These two small parrots are lovebirds, a species in the genus *Agapornis* (from the Greek *agape* ("love") and *ornis* ("bird"). They were named because of their monogamous bonding and because they spend so much time sitting next to one another. (I think the male on the right is turning toward his partner's emotional bid...)

On the next few pages, I offer ideas to get you thinking about lengthening and strengthening the relationship side of your square—whether it's your relationships with your partner, spouse, parent, child, co-worker, friend, or community. There are also several resources that I strongly recommend for further reading.

Recognize the value of emotional intelligence

In his seminal work, *Emotional Intelligence*, Daniel Goleman writes, "Much evidence testifies that people who are emotionally adept—who know and manage their own feelings well, and who read and deal effectively with other people's feelings—are at an advantage in any domain of life."[11] Reading Goleman's book will help you assess your strengths and weaknesses in terms of emotional intelligence, and there are also many effective online tools. But the following questions can get you thinking about the notion of emotional intelligence.

- How good are you at "reading" other people and their interests? How quickly can you adjust your demeanor to best suit the person with whom you're interacting?

- Are you able to recover from a bad interaction or from having pessimistic thoughts, or do these negative situations affect your mood for a long time?

- Do you routinely take on new projects with self-reliance and confidence, or do you typically need an outside deadline or a push from someone else?

- Do you have a strong set of personal convictions, or do you change your attitude and opinions to please other people?

- Can you easily strike up a conversation with someone you've never met, or is that outside of your comfort zone?

Be conscious of bids

Learning more about psychologist John Gottman's work with "emotional bids" can provide incredible insights into your interactions with others. And while Gottman's initial studies focused on married couples, the psychological basis behind "emotional bids" holds true for other key relationships, including siblings, parents and children, work connections, and friendships. In his book *The Relationship Cure: A 5 Step Guide to Strengthening Your Marriage, Family, and Friendships*, Gottman discusses three categories for a person's response to emotional bids:

1. *Turning toward:* A positive, supportive, engaged response that indicates a person's willingness to connect. In relationships where people routinely turn toward each other, they essentially "bank" these positive feelings and can then rely on healthy humor, affection, and trust when inevitable conflict arises.

2. *Turning away:* When a person ignores or avoids a bid for whatever reason—self-centeredness, passive-aggressiveness, boredom—it results in frustration for the bidder. This inevitably erodes a relationship and leads to very few deposits in the "bank" that can sustain the relationship in more difficult times.

3. *Turning against:* A person who reacts with anger, criticism, or sarcasm is moving one step further away and actually punishing another person for making an emotional bid. Gottman explains that once a relationship experiences enough of these types of rejected bids, it leads to feeling of depletion, and one or both of the people begin to give up on "rebidding."

Having an honest conversation—however difficult—with people with whom you are having trouble connecting may go a long way in clarifying and improving your relationship.

Volunteer

There are so many positives to volunteering that it would be impossible to list them all here. But offering compassion and help to others does impact all sides of our square:

- *Relationships:* Volunteering helps twice—it benefits the person or organization who needs the help, and it also benefits the volunteer. Volunteering provides social and emotional rewards, cements feelings of cohesion in a community, and teaches compassion and selflessness to children (and adults!).

- *Physical:* Positions that require physical activity and allow the volunteer to be outside offer healthy rewards for the body, but no matter what the action, the brain benefits. Volunteering has been shown to reduce stress and increase confidence and a sense of well-being for all involved.

- *Spiritual:* Volunteer opportunities frequently center around a religious organization, but regardless of the cause, the experience boosts our connection to our spiritual side by helping us clarify our values and giving us a stronger sense of purpose.

- *Work:* A company that encourages volunteering or sponsors an event can reap practical benefits because it can increase its profile. But much more importantly, co-workers who volunteer can foster important bonds, they have the opportunity to network with like-minded individuals, and they benefit personally by feeling valued.

115

"Everybody can be great. Because anybody can serve. You don't have to have a college degree to serve. You don't have to make your subject and your verb agree to serve…You don't have to know the second theory of thermodynamics in physics to serve. You only need a heart full of grace. A soul generated by love."

— Martin Luther King Jr.

Learn the language of love

And I don't mean Italian (although that certainly wouldn't hurt). In a series of books, counselor and author Gary Chapman explores the specifics of love as if it were a language, one that we need to speak clearly in order to understand and be understood. "My conclusion after thirty years of marriage counseling," he writes, "is that there are five emotional love languages—five ways that people speak and understand emotional love."[12] These are:

1. *Words of affirmation:*
    verbal or written compliments or words of appreciation

2. *Quality time:*
    offering undivided attention and seeking meaningful experiences

3. *Receiving gifts:*
    offering visual symbols of love and thoughtful gifts

4. *Acts of service:*
    doing things that show you care or want to help your partner

5. *Physical touch:*
    acts like holding hands, giving backrubs, hugging, and sharing intimacy

What Chapman points out is that we're often unaware of our own preferred language, yet we get frustrated whenever we feel our partner is not meeting our needs. In addition, we tend to "speak" the language that means most to us, even if it's not the language that our partners prefer. Essentially, says Chapman, "Your emotional love language and the language of your spouse may be as different as Chinese from English." [13] Chapman has an online test to learn more about your love language, and reading his works will teach you how to speak the same language as your partner, your children, and other people critical to maintaining a strong, relationship side of your square.

Draw two squares

Before entering into a serious relationship, talking with your partner about Danforth's square can be an excellent exercise. Take the time to draw your own squares first—without input from each other—and then compare them and have an honest conversation.

- What do each of you think about adding children to the relationship side of your square? Is it important to both of you that one of you stays at home with the kids, or are you on different pages with that?

- How well do you know one another's families? Do you share the same views about the need to live close to one or both of your families, or is this a low priority?

- What are your thoughts on religion and spirituality? If there are very different values or practices, how will you address that?

- Is one of you considering earning a degree or making a possible change in careers? Will you be able to financially support yourselves? Have you taken into consideration the consequences if one or both of your careers demand a great deal of travel?

- Do you share the same feelings about your physical health? If one or both of you need to make lifestyle changes in order to get healthier, will you support each other through that? Do you share at least some interests when it comes to physical activity?

If you find that your squares are completely unaligned, it may indicate trouble with the long-term viability of your relationship. Is there anything you can do to find more alignment? Such conversations can be difficult, but using the four sides of Danforth's square to structure the discussion can be of immense help in determining how you can best align your relationship for more harmony, love, trust, and enjoyment.

Humor, Creativity, and Flow

*The best moments usually occur when a person's
body or mind is stretched to its limits in a voluntary
effort to accomplish something difficult and worthwhile.
...For each person, there are thousands of opportunities
and challenges to expand ourselves.*

— Mihaly Csikszentmihalyi

IN THE PAST FOUR CHAPTERS of this book, I focused on explaining the benefits of lengthening and strengthening each side of our squares—our physical health, our spirituality, our work, and our relationships—in order to find a healthier life balance. My message would be incomplete, however, if I didn't also explore three additional topics: humor, creativity, and a term called "flow." Not only do they connect to all four sides of Danforth's square, but they also have exciting links to neuroscience. Delving into a study of these three topics, therefore, serves to deepen our understanding of what balanced living truly means.

Humor: laughter as medicine

Very early in my surgical career—it was only my fourth or fifth solo surgery—I was ready to scrub in when I realized I hadn't taken off my watch in the locker room. I slid it off my wrist, tied it to the drawstring of my scrub pants, and went about my preparations. The surgery went well, and I was confident as I began to close the patient. Then suddenly, with no warning whatsoever, my baggy scrub pants slid down my legs and dropped in a heap around my ankles. When I heard the thud of my watch hit the floor, I knew its weight must have loosened the drawstring. Like a Scotsman who wears nothing under his kilt, I was left naked from the waist down. Since my hands couldn't leave the sterile field, there was a decidedly awkward moment of silence, followed by an equally awkward question: the head nurse, biting her lower lip to stifle a laugh, asked quietly, "Dr. Maroon, would you like me to pull up your pants?"

It was a horrible moment for me, a person who had been compelled from an early age to take things very seriously and to try and control every situation. So much for the young surgeon maintaining a sense of dignity in his own operating room, right? But seeing the humor in the moment would've been the far better option. How much more respect I would've gotten for laughing with the staff—no harm done because the patient was never in danger, and no one even had a full-frontal view—rather than giving what I recall as my very gruff response and then being gripped with humiliation and defensiveness.

For most of my life, I was a very serious person; humor was juvenile, and I felt I had much more important things to do. And learning to laugh at myself? Not an option. After

We laugh because of the Aha! moment, a reward for our brains when they recognize an incongruity. And because so much of life is made up of such unexpected mismatches—like a surgeon's pants falling down in the operating room—we might as well find humor in their occurrence!

pushing through my depression, however, and understanding the need for greater balance, I gained a real appreciation of what humor and mirth could add to my life, and I became, overall, a more positive person. Simply put, having a healthy sense of humor is precisely that—healthy. And even if you're not naturally outgoing or jovial, a better sense of humor and a more positive attitude can be developed.

It's interesting to think about the basics of the human capacity for humor. Far more than just a knack for telling jokes, humor involves complex neural circuitry including the temporo-occipito-parietal areas, which detect and then resolve the basis of most humor: incongruity. What typically makes something funny, in other words, is a mismatch between what we expect to happen and what actually happens, commonly revealed in a well-timed punch line. Once our brains allow us to cognitively "get the joke," our limbic systems offer up an emotional reaction to the humor, including smiles, laughter, and even tears of joy. Scientists believe laughter predated human language and was a way to express relief when a danger had passed, and some think modern humor shares a similar purpose: we laugh because of the Aha! moment, a reward for the fact that our brains have recognized an incongruity. And because so much of life is made up of such unexpected mismatches—like a surgeon's pants falling down in the operating room—we might as well find humor in their occurrence!

The word humor itself is rooted in an early medical theory. The Latin *umor* refers to bodily liquids, and by the early 1500s, the humors theory of physiology asserted that our mental and physical health was based on the balance of the four primary liquids in our bodies: bile (choleric), black bile (melancholic), phlegm (phlegmatic), and blood (sanguine). If a person had an excess of one "humor" or was lacking in another, he was considered unbalanced or out of temper—from the Latin *temperare*, meaning "mix." This led to humor being used to describe people's moods and whether there was anything odd or eccentric about them, and by the late 1600s, humor had broadened to mean whim and amusement.

Much like Danforth's sides of the square, then, the ancient origins of humor related to balance, and research has proven that humor's modern meaning connects to each side as well. Physically, laughter and a positive mood—even the anticipation of a happy event—have benefits because they relax our bodies by increasing "good" hormones such as endorphins and reducing the "bad" hormones like cortisol and adrenaline. Mentally, seeing situations from a humorous perspective lessens stress and leads to increased creativity and more fluid problem-solving skills. And both socially and spiritually, humor grounds us in the joy of the present, leading to increased altruism, boosting our sense of hope and optimism, and fostering vital connections with friends, spouses, children, and others in a community. A hearty laugh and a shared smile can truly benefit the body, the brain, the heart, and the soul.

Getting to the core of creativity

For many, the adjective "creative" applies only to people who excel in dance, painting, or some other artistic pursuit, and it's often believed people are either born with creativity or they're not. But according to Sir Ken Robinson, an internationally recognized expert on creativity and education, the definition of creativity is "the process of having original ideas that have value."[1] And he laments how this fascinating process, certainly not limited to artists, is so misunderstood that people often fail to appreciate and develop their own innate creative potential.

To better understand that slippery concept of creativity, it's helpful to start with an explanation of our most basic thinking. It all starts with cooperation among neurons, the brain cells that process and transmit information through both electrical and chemical signals. But a single neuron does not hold a single thought. An excellent example offered by the Copenhagen Institute of Neurocreativity is that we have no "apple" neuron. Instead, thinking of an apple activates a wide array of neurons, including sensory neurons that associate with an apple's color, smell, taste, and texture, plus a host of experiential neurons that hold memories and emotions about our previous interactions with apples. A human's ability to think about physical objects or more abstract concepts, therefore, is made possible through a process of gathering, connecting, and analyzing information from various neurons.[2]

And creativity? It's an exciting extension of this very same process. When the neural

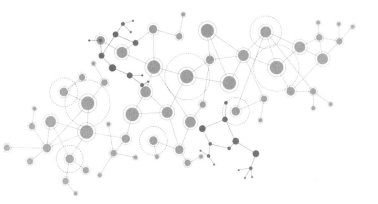

When the neural connections being fired aren't confined to just one object or concept, but instead are blazing new paths and establishing relationships among previously unconnected neurons, it allows for the innovative, inventive thinking we call creativity.

123

connections being fired aren't confined to just one object or concept, but instead are blazing new paths and establishing relationships among previously unconnected neurons, it allows for the innovative, inventive thinking we call creativity. So knowing the human brain contains 100 billion neurons, capable of 100 trillion synaptic connections, in a network over 100 miles long, the potential for creative thought is truly staggering. A long-standing theory held that creativity was housed in only one half of the brain—the right brain/left brain distinction that ascribed creativity to the right hemisphere—but newer findings prove the creative process requires input from the whole brain.

During the creative process, the brain's "imagination" is engaged, stemming from both the hippocampus, the repository for nonemotional memory of fact, as well as from the amygdala, which stores and encodes emotional memories of past experiences. Then the executive network, located in the prefrontal cortex, is called upon to help with problem solving and reasoning. And third, our salience network is busy keeping everything on track, using all the circuits of the brain to process the information and keep the brain focused. So during creative bursts of energy, our emotional reservoir and all the logical elements of thinking are required to make, as Ken Robinson said, "original ideas that have value."

Thinking creatively has never been found to have a direct correlation to a person's IQ, nor does it relate to any specific field of study. Creative thinking occurs in everything from mathematics to art, cooking to teaching, writing to engineering. What is necessary, however, is neuroplasticity, a term that describes the malleability of the brain. We now understand the process of neurogenesis—the birth of new cells—and neuroscience has disproven the long-held belief that our brains become completely "hardwired" after childhood development. So our brains remain "plastic" well into adulthood, able to change at a neural level and even making measurable physical changes as we learn new skills and establish new connections. In an article for *Wired* magazine, Steve Jobs said, "Creativity is just connecting things." Creative thinkers, he continued, were "able to connect experiences they've had and synthesize new things. And the reason they were able to do that was that they've had more experiences or they have thought more about their experiences than other people. Unfortunately, that's too rare of a commodity. A lot of people...don't have enough dots to connect, and they end up with very linear solutions without a broad perspective on the problem."[3]

124

FORMULATING AND PRODUCING creative thoughts is difficult enough, but sadly, insightful, creative ideas can also meet with contempt. Indeed, some of the most creative ideas in history were initially met with scorn or ridicule. Nicolaus Copernicus putting the sun, not Earth, in the center of the universe? Unacceptable. Louis Pasteur linking the spread of disease to germs? Preposterous. Artist Claude Monet painting outside, creating not a realistic depiction but an "impression" of what he saw? Offensive. New ideas are often opposed because they are too different from the norm and threaten the status quo. And in the modern world, even Bill Gates, Steve Jobs, and Mark Zuckerberg had difficultly finding support early on. An appropriate sentiment, one that is typically attributed to nineteenth-century German philosopher Arthur Schopenhauer, is "All truth passes through three stages. First, it is ridiculed. Second, it is violently opposed. Third, it is accepted as being self-evident."

"All truth passes through three stages.
First, it is ridiculed.
Second, it is violently opposed.
Third, it is accepted as being self-evident."

— Arthur Schopenhauer, German philosopher

*Nicolaus Copernicus
and his model of the
heliocentric universe.*

I personally felt pushback on a creative idea early on in my career. I was an assistant resident during a surgery on a patient with a tumor of the cerebellum. It was common practice at the time to perform certain brain surgeries with the patient in an upright position—less bleeding and easier access—but when the lead surgeon unknowingly nicked a thin vein at the back of the brain, air entered it and traveled to the heart, causing a fatal cardiac arrhythmia. This type of air embolus was a recognized problem in neurosurgery, but it was considered rare.

At the time, I was experimenting with a new instrument called an ultrasonic Doppler blood flow meter, designed to calculate the velocity of blood flowing through a vein or artery and used to detect strokes. After this particular patient's death, it occurred to me that this Doppler might be able to detect a difference in sound between a vessel with blood flowing through it and one that contained air. My department chairman allowed me to anesthetize a dog and inject a small amount of air—the same amount that enters a patient being hooked up to an IV; the dog was in no danger—and within a few seconds, the ultrasonic device over the dog's heart made a telltale noise, like a needle scratching a record.

I conducted more research, connecting old ways of doing things with new technology and new possibilities. I then submitted an abstract and was invited to speak to over a thousand neurosurgeons at a national meeting. I presented my findings on the benefits of this ultrasonic technique to detect even a small amount of air as it entered the heart, stating that while the results of this issue were not always fatal, air entered the heart of patients being operated on in the upright position 29 percent of the time. While I thought I would be applauded for my idea, I was instead severely criticized by colleagues, who said my statistics were impossibly high and obviously fabricated. Dr. Michenfelder, then the head of neuroanesthesia at the Mayo Clinic, even personally contacted me to say he was setting out to prove me wrong. He went on to monitor patients using my technique and ultimately did find fault with the data: in his patients, air was discovered not in 29 percent of the cases—but in 31 percent. Doppler detection to determine air embolisms has since become the standard of care when operating in the upright position.

DESPITE THIS TYPE OF PUSHBACK, creativity has unquestionable benefits for all sides of the square. First, creative pursuits that involve trying new skills and "connecting dots" reduces stress on the body, keeps our brains vibrant and healthy, and has even been shown to stem the advance of dementia. Second, in terms of creativity in the workplace, countless studies prove that providing a stimulating environment that encourages cooperative thinking and rewards risk taking can substantially benefit both employer and employee.

Third, nurturing our relationships with intentional creativity—whether that's pursuing common interests with friends, encouraging curiosity and joy through play with a child, or fortifying our commitment to a partner by finding new ways to relate—allows us to continually derive strength from our interactions. The people we care about can be "an elixir of sorts," explains Daniel Goleman in *Social Intelligence*, "an ever-renewing source of energy. ...The practical lesson for us all comes down to: Nourish your social connections."[4]

And finally, creativity can encourage a deeper spiritual life by opening us up to moments of awe, awareness, and joy. But the unique connection between creativity and spirituality can be better explained through an understanding of the final topic to be covered in this chapter: the psychological state of flow.

Learning to go with flow

Professor Mihaly Csikszentmihalyi (me-HIGH cheek-SENT-me-high) is recognized as a pioneer of the positive psychology movement, an uplifting fact in itself considering he witnessed the horrors of World War II as a child in Croatia. When he was confined in an Italian prison during the war, he had his first experience with what he would eventually call "flow": he found that while playing chess, his mind focused on the board in front of him and on his next move, not on his frightening surroundings. He would later determine that it was a combination of the clear rules of the game matched with his competent skills that allowed him to feel an undeniable enjoyment and calmness amidst the chaos.

Years later, Csikszentmihalyi was so inspired by a lecture he heard from Carl Jung in Switzerland that he immigrated to America to study the relatively new discipline of

High

CHALLENGES

Anxiety

Flow Channel

Boredom

Low

Low   SKILLS   High

A different kind of flow chart

Csikszentmihalyi found that when we begin a new activity, we can experience the pleasures of exploration if the challenge is simple enough for us to feel a degree of success. If the challenge is too difficult for our skills, we experience anxiety; if our skills outweigh the challenge, we become bored. The sense of flow, therefore, occurs in the "channel" where we continuously develop our skills to match increasing challenges.[5]

psychology and went on to earn a PhD from the University of Chicago in 1965. Because he had artistic skills, he was personally fascinated with the psychological aspects of creativity—both the intense concentration required in the creative process of painting and the joy and beauty of its unfolding. His seminal book *Flow: The Psychology of Optimal Experience*, published in 1990, moved beyond his exploration of the arts and presented his findings that a "flow" state was indeed a unique combination of intellect and emotion: a point where our skill level and our focus meet a challenge at an ideal intersection. It is here where time seems to fall away, and we revel in how our abilities are rewarded with the unparalleled contentment of being present in the moment.

JUST AS BOTH HUMOR AND CREATIVITY can be explained in neuroscientific terms, we now know that flow engages our brains in incredibly complex ways. When we are in such a focused state, brainwaves change from fast-moving beta waves to the slower-moving alpha and theta waves associated with daydreaming and falling asleep. And our prefrontal cortex—central to self-monitoring and cognitive control—steps out of the way during flow, quieting our doubts and making us more courageous, relaxed, and engaged in the process at hand.

Being in a flow state, therefore, actually rewires our brains, forming new synaptic connections and making specific neural pathways stronger. To borrow a metaphor from poet Robert Frost, the roads that have been "less traveled" in our brains become more habitual choices and are easier to access, made even more enticing by the release of feel-good hormones like dopamine, oxytocin, endorphins, and cannabinoids that accompany the flow state.

Advances in neuroscience allow us to recognize that brains in a state of flow are strikingly similar to brains that have been positively affected by meditation, a practice that offers up a huge array of neurological benefits. Physically, the brain changes during meditation by increasing in volume, and consistent meditation has been shown to result in better long-term brain health. Psychologically, the "me-centered" regions of the brain, which focus on self-referential thinking and can lead to a disorganized monkey mind, are quieted through meditation, allowing the brain to enjoy the sensation of singular thought. Indeed, meditation has positive affects on attention, concentration, and overall well-being, and studies have shown it can help relieve anxiety and depression better and with results lasting far longer than prescribed medication.

Unfortunately, a decidedly "un-flow-like" state has become more common, and is the direct result of the modern notion of multitasking. Those who pride themselves on living permanently in this state—often complaining about the busyness of their lives but actually feeling a sense of superiority because they relate multitasking to success—should know that both their performance and their health are suffering. While the human body can multitask in the sense that we do things like breathe and walk at the same time, a vast difference exists between functions that we can do automatically—breathing, blinking, and some mindless tasks like washing dishes—and those functions that require attention and focus. In short, our brains are actually incapable of multitasking because we can only pay meaningful mental attention to one thing at a time. In a world now known for its sensory clutter, when information, images, and sound bytes vie desperately for our attention around the clock, understanding the benefits of focus and working toward flow states on a regular basis are more important than ever.

HUMOR, CREATIVITY, AND FLOW…three little words with incredibly deep meaning and incalculable possibilities. I'd been a creative thinker earlier in my career, and I could lose myself for hours in a thrilling, challenging surgery or in the complexities of researching new procedures. But I was unappreciative of the actual creative process that was taking place in my brain or of the incredible benefits of what Csikszentmihalyi would soon coin as "flow." I also never went looking for these rewarding experiences in other avenues of my life; work was the only place I felt these meaningful connections, so I placed my entire focus there to become "a success."

When I became painfully aware of the imbalance in my life, however, I realized I'd overlooked the immense rewards associated with the other sides of my square. I've since found true success by taking responsibility for my health and in pursuing creative ways to exercise and eat well, reaping the incredible benefits of flow by setting goals for training with consistency and determination. I've also come to terms with my place in the world by seeking broader experiences, finding more humor, and gaining a sense of calm and acceptance through spiritual practices. And finally, I've continually sought to reap the incomparable benefits of connecting with others—colleagues, my children, my patients, and other adventure seekers—and enjoy the enriching, empowering flow of relationships.

In our life's "toolboxes," three of the most helpful devices are humor, creativity, and flow. They are some of the most reliable sources to help us lengthen and strengthen all four sides of our squares, to deepen our appreciation of what's possible in our lives, and to foster the kind of joy and awe that allow us to become our very best selves. ◻

"It is not the critic who counts; not the man who points out how the strong man stumbles, or where the doer of deeds could have done them better. The credit belongs to the man who is actually in the arena, whose face is marred by dust and sweat and blood; who strives valiantly; who errs, who comes short again and again, because there is no effort without error and shortcoming; but who does actually strive to do the deeds; who knows great enthusiasms, the great devotions; who spends himself in a worthy cause; who at the best knows in the end the triumph of high achievement, and who at the worst, if he fails, at least fails while daring greatly, so that his place shall never be with those cold and timid souls who neither know victory nor defeat."[6]

— Theodore Roosevelt, excerpt from the speech
"Citizenship in a Republic," delivered at the Sorbonne
in Paris, France, on April 23, 1910

The Square for Kids

My own self, at my very best, all the time.

— Motto for American Youth Foundation camps

YOU MIGHT SAY I LEARNED the importance of balancing my life during that tumultuous year I spent in Bridgeport, Ohio. But that doesn't go far enough. The fact of the matter is, picking up that copy of Danforth's *I Dare You* was actually the first time I understood the very notion of balanced living in the first place. And the four-square living model was so simple in its presentation and so clear in its benefits that it has helped guide me ever since.

But I was in my forties when I picked up that book! I had already spent such a large part of my life out of balance—not focusing on my health, not prioritizing my relationships, placing little value on spirituality, not living by any deeply held morals—that imbalance had unfortunately come to feel completely normal. In the introduction to this book, I wrote that I'm now grateful for the brutal events I experienced during that difficult year because they gave me a much-needed wake-up call. But what a gift it would've been to have understood the value of balance earlier in my life! How much better to never have "fallen asleep" in the first place, to have been awake and alert all along to the rich possibilities of the four-square way of thinking.

This last chapter, therefore, could be considered the most important one in this book because its goal is to adapt and reshape the material I've covered so it relates to youth. If parents, grandparents, teachers, or anyone who spends time with children and adolescents can consider balance in this new light, they will see the undeniable benefits of discussing Danforth's square early and often with the next generation. In *I Dare You*, Danforth spoke to youths very directly—addressing his statements to "young men," "young women," and even "barefoot boys on the farm"—and in his preface, he wrote that "a proven four-fold program, plus a love for Youth, plus an inner urge—all *dare* me to write this book."[1]

Some people may consider the concept of Danforth's square too philosophical or too difficult to get across to a young person, but nothing could be further from the truth. The simple square makes for an easy visual metaphor, and labeling each side with Danforth's four categories in relatable terms makes it an incredibly effective tool.

How we can
take care of our
health

How we can
make the most of
our brains

How we
can fill our lives
with meaning

How we can
show other people we
care about them

When these concepts are presented consistently and become part of a family's lexicon, they foster the kind of routines and habits that can shape a child's future path. The desired effect is that by helping young people celebrate the importance of each individual side of the square and understand how interrelated these sides are to one another, we promote a natural desire for balance. And the more intrinsic this desire becomes—the more children recognize that paying attention to these things offers its own continuous reward—the more they will experience the true benefits of balance: good health, positive relationships, and a sense of flow as they discover their strengths and purpose.

Strengthening a child's physical side

Forty years ago, even 20 years ago, a book like this wouldn't need to specifically address any serious children's physical health issues. Basic pediatric advice back then reminded parents to make sure their children were eating their vegetables and getting plenty of fresh air, and then they moved on to discuss sleep habits and the pros and cons of pacifiers. Today, however, we are facing the serious issue of childhood obesity, which has reached epidemic proportions.

135

According to 2014 reports from the Centers for Disease Control, obesity has more than doubled in children and has quadrupled in adolescents in the past 30 years. As of 2012, more than a third of children and adolescents were overweight or obese. The CDC attributes this to "caloric imbalance"—when not enough calories are expended to offset calories consumed—and recognizes that these health issues are affected by genetic, behavioral, and environmental factors.[2] So parents and caregivers must take responsibility for providing healthy food options, establishing good exercise habits, and taking steps to safeguard their children from pollutants, pesticides, and artificial food ingredients.

And now I'll say exactly what you're thinking: that's all much easier said than done. Yes, it is. Young children will not suddenly stop eating french fries and spend less time playing video games on the couch just because their parents explain epigenetics and nutrigenomics to them. Plus, the food that they shouldn't be consuming is everywhere, displayed in pretty packages purposely designed to attract their attention. And the information about our food choices and our environment—food additives, organic food options, low-fat versus high-fat foods, air pollutants—can be overwhelming for even the most dedicated parent.

But to simplify the issue of children's health, I'll repeat the advice I offered for adults from chapter 5: it comes down to eating as many healthy whole foods as possible, making movement enjoyable rather than a chore, and learning the incredible value of good habits. First, children are profoundly affected by what they are exposed to, so if they have steady access to chips, sodas, and fast food, this will almost inevitably become their norm. Similarly, if they're not given fun opportunities to run, move, play, and learn new skills, this also leads to a sedentary lifestyle. When they see healthy choices modeled by parents, however, or they witness a family member making successful changes to their diet and exercise routines, they may still grumble and complain, but they're ultimately more likely to adopt those habits themselves. The essential lesson to teach children is that long-term good health is the result of simple, consistent, and smart choices rather than fad diets, diet pills, or grueling exercise.

The last piece of the puzzle here is actually psychological. Our children are growing up in a time that seems to be all about convenience and speed, which has denied them the patience that good health habits often require. Why prepare foods from scratch when you can grab a burger from the drive-through window or heat up a frozen meal in the microwave? This rush also means children don't learn to appreciate processes, like how food actually grows, how to prepare healthy food, or what happens to their bodies when they don't take care of them.

We've also reached a near obsession with ensuring our kids have high self-esteem about their bodies, and ironically, the results are dangerous. While promoting a "love yourself the way you are" attitude is certainly beneficial to counter the ads filled with unnaturally skinny, airbrushed models, many children—and especially teens—now accept being overweight as okay and perfectly normal. And trying to discuss weight with children can instantly make them feel as though they're being shamed or judged.

"Childhood obesity has become a big issue for family physicians," says pediatrician

Perhaps the ultimate goal is to help children and adolescents focus not on the weight of their bodies and how they look, but on the health of their bodies and how they feel. In short, healthy feels good. If this becomes the mantra related to the physical side of a child's square, it can lead to a lifetime of joy and well-being.

Jamie McNanie of Pittsburgh. "My job is to guide a child toward healthy living, but when I broach the subject with parents whose child is overweight, they often dismiss my concerns." Jamie says some parents deny there's anything wrong with their child, while other parents believe that since several members of their family are overweight, it's genetic and just inevitable that the child is overweight, too. Jamie recognizes that tight food budgets, access to fresh foods, and irregular childcare are just a few of the issues that can complicate the matter. She has seen cases of real success, however, when parents can look beyond the immediate weight issue of their child and recognize the need to change the family's lifestyle and exercise habits long-term. "Increasing activity levels, buying and preparing healthier foods, switching from soda to water and milk," says Jamie, "are all habits that will benefit not only the child but everyone in the family."[3]

Perhaps the ultimate goal is to help children and adolescents focus not on the weight of their bodies and how they look, but on the health of their bodies and how they feel. In short, healthy feels good. It this can become the mantra related to the physical side of a child's square, it can lead to a lifetime of joy and well-being.

Tending to the spiritual

An author broaching the issue of how parents should address spirituality with their children is arguably more awkward than a pediatrician bringing up the issue of obesity, but what an important issue it is. While I was raised in a Catholic family and continue to find solace by returning to those roots, I have also gained wisdom and immense respect by learning about the rituals and philosophies of other religions and spiritual practices. In a similar light, William H. Danforth was a Christian, and the American Youth Foundation was originally a Christian-based organization. Over time, however, the AYF shifted its focus away from the particulars of any one religion to the broader benefits of encouraging children to have compassion, strong morals and ethics, and a continuously developing sense of purpose.

In chapter 6, I included an illustration that showed Simon Sinek's concentric circles, with the *whats* and *hows* of things on the outer rings, and the all-important *why* at the center. Sinek's point was that only by asking difficult *why* questions can we define our lives beyond the stages of simply knowing facts, processes, and procedures. It's no coincidence, then, that young children naturally formulate strings of *why* questions when trying to make sense of all the information their brains gather during bursts of development. What they're seeking is true understanding. They will rephrase questions and ask follow-ups until they receive an answer that satisfies their insatiable curiosity, quite often to the exasperation of their parents!

Many situations can be explained to children relatively simply, including why they shouldn't run with scissors or keep pet frogs under their pillows. But it's the big *Whys*—those with a capital W, about origins and endings, rights and wrongs, and the inexplicable beauty of butterflies—that bring up the need for children to have access to a way of thinking that takes them beyond themselves and allows them to feel safe wrestling with concepts that cannot always be seen or proven. Whether parents guide their child along the path of an organized religion or choose instead to offer consistent ethical and spiritual teachings, the purpose is to help young people develop habits of conscience that will then provide them with a moral compass, one they can use to navigate life's inevitable challenges and adversities.

In their book *Raising Resilient Children: Fostering Strength, Hope, and Optimism in Your Child*, psychologists Robert Brooks and Sam Goldstein address the importance of nurturing a resilient mindset in children by allowing them to solve their own problems, to learn from their mistakes, and to recognize how their actions impact others. "When children are enlisted in helping others and engaging in responsible behaviors," they write, "we communicate our trust in them and faith in their ability to handle a variety of tasks. ...As children develop this foundation of a resilient mindset and develop responsibility, a commitment to be accountable for one's life emerges."[4]

And it's this accountability, a commitment to being one's best self for the good of everyone, that lies at the heart of spirituality. Volunteering in the community, attending religious services, creating family traditions to offer gratitude, exploring spiritual traditions of the world through art, music, and literature—all allow children to find comfort, seek beauty, and acknowledge and celebrate the spiritual sides of their lives.

139

Volunteering in the community, attending religious services, creating family traditions to offer gratitude, exploring spiritual traditions of the world through art, music, and literature—all allow children to find comfort, seek beauty, and acknowledge and celebrate the spiritual sides of their lives.

Developing healthy relationships

As I mentioned in chapter 7, healthy relationships are often our greatest source of joy. But developing and maintaining these connections is an ongoing, often difficult challenge—even for adults—because relationships involve emotions and ever-changing dynamics. But when you factor in the complex stages of children's emotional and cognitive development, and later the radical, unpredictable changes that occur during puberty, it can be overwhelming to know how best to help our children navigate the prickly path through their social world.

For younger children, author and psychologist Eileen Kennedy-Moore suggests fostering three key processes: seeing, thinking, and doing. First, because good social skills involve recognizing cues, adults can point out what children should look for when entering a social situation, including the emotions they see on people's faces. When it comes to thinking, the key is to model good problem-solving skills and talk about seeing things from other people's point of view. And to increase confidence in social situations, children can benefit from rehearsing what to do. Simple etiquette—looking people in the eye, not interrupting, learning to ask and answer questions—may seem to be on the brink of extinction in this age. Yet it allows children the opportunity to interact with adults to make and maintain friendships.[5]

140

A point of view

In Harper Lee's *To Kill a Mockingbird,* a young Scout Finch struggles to find her place in a new school and to navigate her expanding social world in America during the 1930s, including issues of class and race. Her father Atticus' response? "First of all," he said, "if you can learn a simple trick, Scout, you'll get along a lot better with all kinds of folks. You never really understand a person until you consider things from his point of view…until you climb into his skin and walk around in it."[6]

But no matter how masterful children are during their elementary years, anyone can be thrown for a violent loop as puberty hits. Boys' main growth hormone, testosterone, increases nearly 20 times over the course of a few years, affecting their ability to control their emotions, especially anger, aggression, and attraction. And wild fluctuations in estrogen have profound effects on girls' levels of serotonin, the chemical that balances mood. These ebbs and flows of emotion are part of what keeps young people on relationship roller coasters with their friends, parents, and siblings.

Another factor in emotional teen turbulence is the variable time for maturation of the adolescent brain. Myelin is the "insulation" that covers every nerve cell in the brain to enable optimal functioning, but different parts of the brain become myelinated or insulated at different times. The frontal lobes reach maturity and insulation last, typically earlier in girls than in boys, and since this region of the brain governs the emotions, acting out and poor emotional control can be common until full brain maturation occurs, somewhere in the early twenties.

While this chemical and maturational flux has always presented complications, modern tweens and teens are facing something no other generation has faced before: ever-present technology—the good, the bad, and the downright ugly. Cell phones allow them constant access to everything on the Internet, texting allows for unprecedented communication, and many social media sites give them, literally, a world audience. Are there benefits? Of course. Technology offers collaboration among peers, opportunities to share fun photos, and the ability to stay in touch with lots of people, to name just a few positives. The drawbacks, however, are also considerable. Cyberbullying, access to inappropriate material that taints relationships, and a dangerous underestimation of the public nature of technology means kids can get themselves into trouble, sometimes very seriously.

In her book *It's Complicated: The Social Lives of Networked Teens,* social media researcher and professor Danah Boyd presents a map of the new frontier of parenting in a tech-heavy world. With over 80 percent of teens now owning cell phones—and roughly half owning smartphones—her overall message is that parents need to accept the reality of the new situation, working along with their children to focus on the benefits of technology and avoid the pitfalls. "The ability to understand how context, audience, and identity intersect is one of the central challenges people face in learning how to navigate social media," Boyd writes. "And, for all the mistakes they can and do make, teens are often leading the way at figuring out how to navigate a networked world in which collapsed contexts and imagined audiences are par for the course."[7]

Continuously lengthening and strengthening the relationship side of the square is certainly daunting for children. But we can count on Danforth again to put the challenge in its simplest terms. When advising his readers about maintaining relationships, he begins with the importance of working on ourselves first. "Personality," he writes, "is a vague, intangible thing to talk about on paper. But how real, how tremendous it is in life all around us!" He then asserts that it's the most basic things—thoughtfulness, kindness, compassion, gratitude, and finding joy—that we can use to create that personality.[8]

142

Children at work (and play)

I have already covered the importance of adults finding a balance between their work lives and their personal lives. But children and adolescents must also learn to juggle requirements—homework, chores, sports practice, and perhaps part-time jobs—with what I'll call the "joys of youth." And it's a very critical balancing act: too much time focused on only serious matters means children can suffer from the same unhealthy side effects of stress as adults. Not enough focus, however, means they can squander opportunities that would've led to more meaningful, purposeful futures. What's a parent to do?

It seems instinctual for adults to buoy children up and give them the confidence necessary for successful pursuits, so many parents and teachers have taken to praising children every chance they get. This "you're so smart" approach—including superfluous sticker charts and giving trophies to every ball player, even those on the losing team—certainly seems kind; how could praise be bad for a child? As it turns out, however, slathering praise on children actually has detrimental effects, unless we praise them for the right things.

Here's why. In her seminal work *Mindset: The New Psychology of Success*, psychology professor Carol Dweck presents significant research on two entirely different types of thinking. Fixed mindset people, she explains, assume success is a result of intelligence and innate abilities; they feel effort is only necessary if one doesn't display enough talent. Alternately, growth mindset people view success as a result of working hard, taking risks, developing an array of talents, and having a strong sense of purpose and determination. Dweck found that while people with either mindset can find success, those with a fixed mindset often pay a dear price.

"In one world—the world of fixed traits—success is about proving you're smart or talented. Validating yourself," Dweck writes. "In the other—the world of changing qualities—it's about stretching yourself to learn something new. Developing yourself."[9] By constantly telling our children they are smart, therefore, and praising them on outcomes, we set them up to assume a fixed mindset. When that "very smart" child begins to struggle with math or the "superstar athlete" experiences defeat, they are ill equipped to solve the problem or redirect their efforts, so they often blame others, act out, or give up.

Children praised regularly for process and effort, however, learn to view adversity from a far healthier perspective because they connect their actions, and not their entire identity,

In praise of less praise

Po Bronson, the coauthor of *Nurture Shock: New Thinking About Children*, says praise has become something of a "panacea for the anxieties of modern parenting," and he recognized that he needed to pull back on the broad praise he lavished on his young son. Instead, he had conversations with him about the good things that result when we have to struggle through tough times. Wanting to review his message, he asked his son, "What happens to your brain again, when it gets to think about something hard?" And his son responded, without hesitation, "It gets bigger, like a muscle."[10]

American Youth Foundation

Scotsman John L. Alexander, who had previously worked with both the Boy Scouts and the YMCA, became AYF's first executive director in 1925. It was Alexander who formulated the motto, "My own self, at my very best, all the time," seen here crowning the stone fireplace in Camp Merrowvista's dining hall. For over 90 years, AYF camps, year-round programs, and conferences have dared young people to "aspire nobly, adventure daringly, and serve humbly," and their simple logo feature initials that represent the four sides of Danforth's original square: social, mental, religious, and physical.

to the outcome. Dweck's studies show that kids who hear supportive words like "What an interesting drawing! How did you choose those colors?" become far more engaged in their learning and are more willing to take on challenges than those who hear unrealistic praise like "You're the best artist ever!" Dweck writes, "The growth mindset does allow people to love what they're doing—and to continue to love it in the face of difficulties."[11]

And this is where Dweck intersects at an interesting point with Ken Robinson. Robinson's notion of finding an "Element," as described in chapter 7, is about embracing natural proclivities and talents, which seems to fall more on the side of having a fixed mindset. But his true desire is to dispense with the factory-style approach to education and to help people, especially young people, become aware of the exciting dynamic nature of their abilities and recognize the work that is involved in developing them. Indeed, Robinson thinks the question "How intelligent are you?" should always be replaced with "How are you intelligent?" and that effort, passion, and purpose—the traits of the open mindset—are the true definitions of success.[12]

This is a healthy way for children to lengthen and strengthen the work side of their square in preparation for whatever they choose to pursue as adults. While kids often complain about having to walk the dog or empty the trash, and no child floats blissfully through every school subject, the biggest gift we can give them is the knowledge that their efforts matter and that we will be there, sitting in the front row, as they figure out their passions and purpose in life.

I HAVE BEEN QUOTING William H. Danforth and his philosophies throughout this book, but it's critical in this chapter to emphasize Danforth's unwavering dedication to youth. In addition to creating the Ralston-Purina Company and working with his wife, Adda, to start the Danforth Foundation, Danforth also joined forces with organizational leaders from the Boy Scouts and the YMCA to start the American Youth Foundation (AYF) in the early 1920s. In 1925, the AYF began operating two summer programs: Camp Merrowvista, set on over 600 acres in scenic New Hampshire; and Camp Miniwanca, which includes 360 acres of woodlands along the shores of Lake Michigan. Both were based on the concept of "four-fold living" and still flourish today, with year-round camps and on-site and off-site leadership training.

Anna Kay Vorsteg, the current president and CEO of the American Youth Foundation, has witnessed firsthand the tremendous benefits Danforth's square has offered to children and teens, and she always looks forward to working with new and returning campers at both the Merrowvista and Miniwanca sites. "The four-fold concept provides the structure for our camps and is such a great metaphor for our kids," she explains from a rocking chair on the wraparound porch of the Big House at Camp Merrowvista. "They can think of the spiritual side of the square as their wiring, what makes them tick. Then their mental and physical sides are their resources, which they can continually develop. And then, because they've put in all that work and understand what it means to be their 'own best self,' they can forge some really great relationships."[13]

And she's not kidding. Many parents of current campers attended AYF programs when they were younger, and because the camp had such a profound influence on their lives, they make it a priority to enroll their own children. Several even met their future spouses as teen campers. And while the majority of the campers come from nearby states, many others travel across the country or from other continents to attend the programming each year.

One parent used the phrase "insatiable joy" to describe her daughter's experiences at Camp Merrowvista over the years and said the camp was her daughter's second home. "There are, of course, lots of camps that offer good opportunities for children," she said. "But the philosophy here runs so deep that the kids really sense the history of the place." And that philosophy and history linger long after summer camp is over. When asked about whether she followed the four-fold living concept during the school year, a camper named Hannah said it undoubtedly made her more conscious of her habits and of the choices she made. And she was not alone. Other campers agreed that while they could get overwhelmed with schoolwork or lazy about their health, thinking about their square helped them recognize why they were feeling out of balance and allowed them to get back on track.

"If a challenge strengthens, tests, and awakens a child to their capacities and ultimately to the best in themselves or the best in another, it likely builds self-reliance and readiness for life's path and therefore it holds an important place in AYF programming."

— Anna Kay Vorsteg

While the AYF camps have deep historical roots, Director Anna Kay keeps her eye on modern issues that affect current campers. In a letter she posted on the website just before the start of 2016 summer programs, for instance, she addressed the worrisome trend of parents and institutions trying to overprotect children, resulting in insulation from adversity and negative consequences. "It seems adults have slipped into patterns that are aimed at smoothing and readying the path before the child," she writes, "more than readying the child for whatever obstacles lie in the path before them." While the AYF certainly respects and addresses issues like food allergies and offensive language, it remains "an institution that nurtures by challenge" and focuses on empowering campers to rely on themselves and their peers to solve problems. "If a challenge strengthens, tests, and awakens a child to their capacities and ultimately to the best in themselves or the best in another," Anna Kay writes, "it likely builds self-reliance and readiness for life's path and therefore it holds an important place in AYF programming." [14]

In *I Dare You*, Danforth wrote about spending time at Camp Miniwanca in Michigan and recognizing that the campers were participating happily and fully in every activity he saw. "These young people have realized that all sides of life can be equally interesting," he commented. "They are daring to live at their best, following a Four-square program, and they are having a glorious time doing it."[15] ◻

" These young people have realized that all sides of life can be equally interesting. They are daring to live at their best, following a Four-square program, and they are having a glorious time doing it."

— William H. Danforth

Where else could that divinity be hiding?

In Danforth's *I Dare You*, one of his chapters is titled "I Dare You to Build Character" and includes a charming Hindu story about humans and a missed opportunity. The story explains how all men on earth were once gods, but when they abused their power, the divine Brahma took away their spirituality and rich knowledge, intending to hide it where none of them could ever find it again. One thought was to bury it deep inside the earth. "No," said Brahma, shaking his head. "Man will simply dig down and find it." Another thought was to sink it into the ocean. "No," Brahma said. "Man will one day learn to dive and would find it there as well." Someone else suggested they place it on top of a high mountain, but again, Brahma disagreed: "Man will eventually be able to climb every mountain on earth." Finally, after considerable thought, Brahma made a decision. "We will place divinity inside of every human," he announced. "I'm sure they will never think to look there."[16]

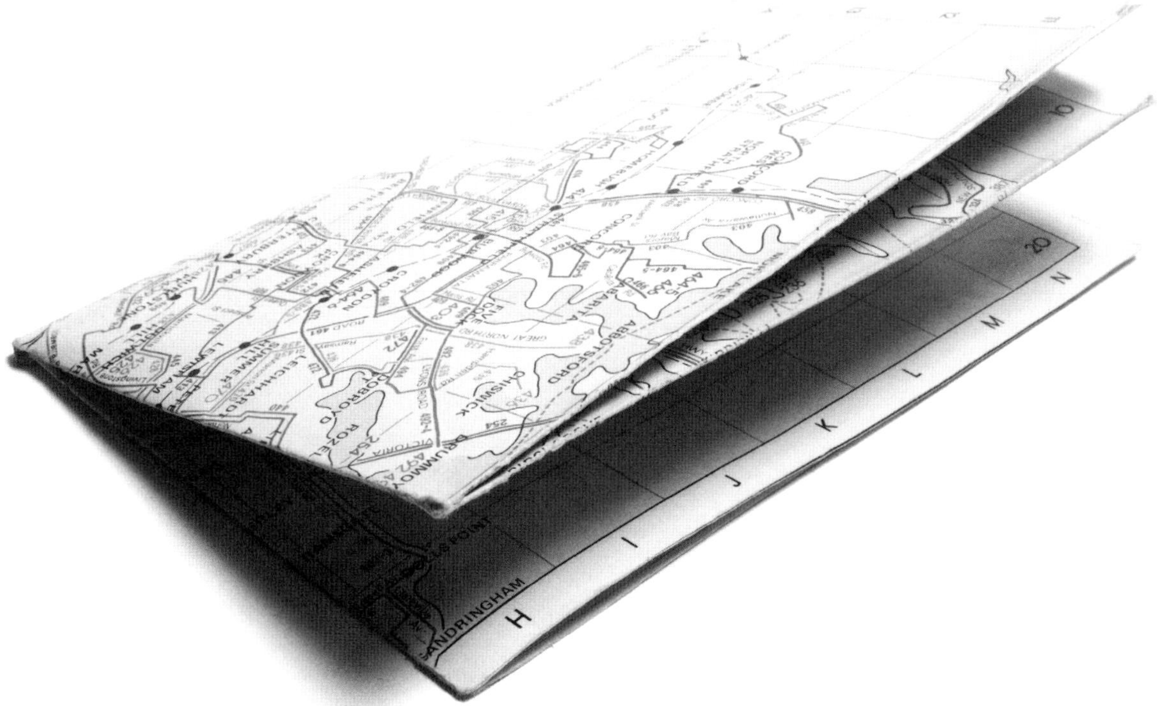
ABBOTSFORD
SANDRINGHAM
H
I
J
K
L
M
N
20
10

From Start to Summit

Climb the mountain not to plant your flag,
but to embrace the challenge, enjoy the air, and behold the view.
Climb it so you can see the world, not so the world can see you.

— David McCullough Jr.

I CHOSE, early in my life, to climb the metaphorical mountain of a profession. And I believed for a long time that the most important thing I could do was to reach its summit. But I began this journey without a reliable map and without the supplies I would ultimately need. That's why, after reaching a peak of success in my early forties, I somehow ended up at a truck stop, feeling panic rather than accomplishment. "Where *am* I?" I thought, utterly stupefied. "And why am I here *alone?*"

The only map I'd used contained a single straight line up the mountain, without any information on the beautiful vistas I could have been paying attention to, alternative routes I could have tried, or crevasses I should have avoided. The map also didn't have any key at the bottom with concentric circles and the word "Why?" written in the center, something Simon Sinek—mentioned in chapter 6—thinks all maps need. And the supply I needed most of all was my own health. Without it, I ended up dangerously out of shape, physically, mentally, and spiritually.

The other serious mistake I made when trekking up the mountain of success was not recognizing the benefits of having good traveling companions. While my IQ was high enough to allow me to reach professional heights, I remained ignorant about my emotional intelligence. I hadn't fostered vibrant, healthy relationships, and as any hiker knows, climbing solo can be a very dangerous thing.

It's hard for me to believe it's been over three decades since I spent that year in Bridgeport. In the intervening years, I've returned to a profession I love, but I've also learned how important it is to find success outside of that realm. Have I faltered and found myself out of balance since then? Absolutely. But William H. Danforth's square is everpresent in my mind, and I can recite by heart a passage from his *I Dare You*—the quote that introduced this book's preface: "You have not one, but four lives to live—a four-fold opportunity to grow. A body, a brain, a heart, and a soul—these are our living tools. To use them is not a task. It is a golden opportunity."[1]

I had what can only be described as a golden opportunity to test the strength of all four sides of my square when I got a phone call from my close friend Rajesh Durbal in the fall of 2013. He'd been looking for a way to raise awareness for his charitable Live Free Foundation, so he came up with the idea for a "No Limits Tour." He planned to make visits to several orphanages in Africa and give inspirational talks in several cities, and he wanted his trip to culminate with a trek up Mount Kilimanjaro—the tallest free-standing mountain in the world at 19,331 feet. He intended to climb with a group of other amputees and spur them on with the motto, "Your attitude determines your altitude." Oh, and by the way, "Dr. Joe, could you come with us and serve as our team's doctor?"

I was 74 at the time, had only hiked a few trails around Pittsburgh, and honestly thought Rajesh was a little crazy to ask. But when I mentioned it to my daughter Isabella, then 18 and a freshman in college, she immediately said, "Dad, let's do it!" Still apprehensive but thinking of "attitude and altitude," I accepted the challenge. Bella and I set aside time to train together in the months leading up to the trip, including repeated climbs of the stairway of the University of Pittsburgh's Cathedral of Learning…all 764 steps. And then on February 19, 2014, after a 20-hour flight from Pittsburgh, we landed in Tanzania and bonded immediately with our incredible team.

I was 74 at the time, had only hiked a few trails around Pittsburgh, and honestly thought Rajesh was a little crazy to ask. But when I mentioned it to my daughter Isabella, then 18 and a freshman in college, she immediately said, "Dad, let's do it!"

The climbers from South Africa included Heugene, 38, a former high-security prison guard who was 225 pounds of muscle and towered over me at 6'2". He'd lost his leg above the knee after an unnecessary and poorly performed surgery that was supposed to treat a calf injury. And Kevin, 29, a computer operator, who at the age of 20 crashed his car after swerving to avoid hitting a cat. He woke up from an induced coma and learned he'd lost his right leg below the knee. Another car accident left Zizi, who'd been on the path to becoming a professional rugby player, without a left leg. And a man nicknamed Irish was thrown from a car at the age of four and suffered severe nerve damage in his left arm, rendering it unusable. Finally, Dylan, just 21, was born with phocomelia, a rare disease that left him without arms but with deformed hands attached near his shoulders. All five of these men had faced profound adversity in their lives, and many had been brutally teased for being disabled. But now all are successful and healthy, and all participate in competitive sports, proving just how "able" they are.

In addition to my daughter, two other women joined our climb. Nicolene, born in Namibia, had dealt with more than her share of adversity. After her mother abandoned her family, she grew up with an abusive father and was molested by a teacher at boarding school. This stunning woman later traveled throughout Europe as a model and was about to sign with Victoria's Secret when she gave up that career to become a sports therapist and an athlete who works to raise awareness for important causes. She's also a devoted mother

153

to her young daughter and says, "It's an opportunity to mother myself, to be the kind of mom I never had." And then there was Lee, who hails from Zurich and is a world-class body builder. Growing up, she had to wear heavy boots to straighten her legs, but she'd sneak out her window at night without them to teach herself how to run, and she has since become an elite athlete. Because her sister was born intellectually challenged, and her own son had to recover from a severe injury when he was only nine, Lee devotes much of her life to helping others and is the founder of the Guts 2 Glory Foundation. In fact, it was her connection to Rajesh that brought all of us together for the Mount Kilimanjaro trek.[2]

For six days, we made our way along the Rongai route, which ascends from the northeastern side of Kilimanjaro, along the border between Tanzania and Kenya. We were in an almost constant state of flow, stretching ourselves to pursue a single, very visible goal—the snow-covered summit we could always see in the distance. Over the rough terrain, up through the decreasing air supply, and in subfreezing temperatures, we all dealt with significant pain, yet my blisters and old legs were nothing compared to the bleeding stumps of the amputees. It was the strength of our relationships, the awesome beauty that surrounded us, and our empathy and humor that kept us moving and motivated.

Dylan, for example, awkwardly lugged a golf club all the way up the mountain, determined to drive a golf ball off the summit using the stumps of his arms—which he accomplished, quite triumphantly! And after Heugene's legs sank into a snowbank, and his

Despite the challenges, we were motivated by the near absurdity of what our peculiar little group was trying to do. We had come together from all parts of the world and were stubbornly determined to climb the highest mountain in Africa.

next step left his prosthesis buried, we went about helping him dig out his leg and laughed the whole time. Despite the challenges, we were motivated by the near absurdity of what our peculiar little group was trying to do. A mix of young and old, most missing a limb (or two or three), we had come together from all parts of the world and were stubbornly determined to climb the highest mountain in Africa.

The entire experience—from start to summit—allowed me to examine each side of my square. I was performing my role as a doctor and even had to deliver the heartbreaking news to Irish that he had to be sent back down the mountain after becoming seriously ill from contaminated water. I was challenging myself physically, moving one step at a time from the 95-degree heat of a rainforest to sub-zero temperatures at the peak. And I was strengthening my relationship with my daughter Bella and sharing the experience with a group of committed, inspiring, and honorable human beings. And spiritually? Being able to look down from the summit to the plains of the Serengeti, and then glance up to see the sun and the moon on opposite sides of the sky—that turned out to be an ideal spot from which to count all of my blessings.

HINDSIGHT ALLOWS ME to marvel at how I went from lying in bed in a tiny farmhouse along the border of West Virginia to standing on the summit of Mount Kilimanjaro, and this book gave me an opportunity to reflect on my long journey to a balanced life. By scrutinizing the adversities I faced—as a neurosurgeon, husband, father, athlete, and human being—and following them to their roots, I can now clearly see the hard-earned solutions.

Hippocrates, known as the Father of Medicine, is credited with the quote, "I will prevent diseases whenever I can, for prevention is preferable to cure." I'd spent the majority of my years so focused on curing problems associated with the brain and spine, on "fixing" other people, that I didn't think much about preventing their problems in the first place. And I certainly didn't spend enough time trying to prevent my own problems; for years, I had no insight into the atrophy of my physical health, my spiritual well-being, or my relationships. I lived wildly out of balance because my work life was so disproportionate to every other side of my square.

"It is not about conquering the mountain, it is about conquering yourself."

— Sir Edmund Hillary, *View from the Summit*

The photo above is the peak of Mount Kilimanjaro, the highest freestanding mountain in the world. And to the left are my climbing companions at the summit: Dylan, Zizi, Rajesh, Lee, and Kevin are standing, and Nicolene, Bella, and Heugene are in the front (holding up a Pittsburgh Steelers banner, no less!).

My hope in writing this book is to offer as much preventative medicine as possible, or at the very least some real-life cures to the sensory overload and burnout so prevalent in today's world. While I've been hesitant to share my personal experiences in written form—revealing my weaknesses that are often, frankly, embarrassing—I was encouraged when I read the following words in *Reaching Out*, a book by priest and professor Henri Nouwen: "My life belongs to others just as much as it belongs to me….What is experienced as most unique often proves to be most solidly embedded in the common condition of being human."[3] My specific story is unique to my life, of course, but my experiences are indeed "embedded" in the shared human journey.

The simple notion of the square set forth by William H. Danforth is the best metaphor I've ever come across for achieving balance in the midst of our unpredictable, amazing, and sometimes frightening lives. The successful programs of the American Youth Foundation are a testament to Danforth's approach, and when I've spoken on the topic of balance to fellow physicians, I can see how strongly it resonates with my audience. I only hope my exploration of the square will serve as a reliable map to help you avoid the pitfalls on the roads you are traveling. And the square may even serve as the foundation for a necessary rebuilding, as it was for me when I was hurt and sorry and questioning the very value of my life.

Now solidly in my fourth quarter, I look back over a life scarred by depression and divorce, and by the death of a beloved son and both of my parents. But that is juxtaposed against the positive experiences of trying my best to help thousands of patients with surgery and treatment; the excitement of competing internationally as an athlete and appreciating the remarkable benefits of good health; the joys of learning how to build positive relationships with family and friends; and the peace of attaining a more balanced life. The climbers who ascended Mount Kilimanjaro with me recognized their adversities and overcame them in order to succeed. That, simply stated, is what we all must do when we face mountains, whether they are literal or metaphorical. I've learned the value of balanced living, and now I dare you—as William Danforth dared me—to do the same. ◻

I WANT TO USE THESE VALUABLE PAGES to acknowledge two groups of people: first, those who've helped me personally and professionally on my journey through life, and then those whose contributions helped me create the book you now hold in your hands.

From an early age, I learned important lessons on the athletic field, so I thank every coach I've had—from grade school through college—for positive encouragement and for teaching me how to handle both victory and defeat on the fields of friendly strife.

And beginning with the Sisters of Charity, from first through twelfth grade, religion and spirituality have affected my thinking and actions. I've tried to do good things in my life—not always successfully, I know—but I'm deeply appreciative for all those teachers and mentors who have done their best to keep me on track.

To the thousands of patients I've treated over the years, I know that I have, at times, been a wounded healer. But doing my best to help those who are confronting life-threatening tumors, painful disabilities, or brain and spinal cord injuries has required me to give of myself in a way that seems to transfer energy and ultimately works to heal us both. So a sincere thank you for placing such trust in me and allowing me to be a partner in your lives.

To my colleagues—notably Jeff Bost, Matt El-Kadi, Adnan Abla, Vince Miele, Dade Lunsford, Robert Friedlander, Paul Gardner, Carl Snyderman, Julian Bailes, Anthony Yates, Mark Duca, Jim Bradley, Jack Kennerdell, John Moossy, and John Norwig—the lessons I've learned from you, both technically and personally, are appreciated more than you know. And I couldn't do what I do without the expertise of my nurses and assistants, Tammy Albaugh, Marsha Austin, Bambi Hilliard, Michelle Wink, and Sarah Ketterman.

My thanks to Mark Lovell and Micky Collins, both brilliant neuropsychologists, for their academic acumen and their tenacity while we worked together to develop the neurocognitive ImPACT test, which has improved athletic concussion identification and management worldwide. The two of them remained supportive through some rough times, and I am grateful to both of them for their friendship.

I also want to acknowledge the support provided by Michael Puskar, Robert Coury and the Mylan Foundation, Nelson and Claudia Peltz, Dennis and Rose Heindl, Lewis Topper, Nan Cameron, Shirley Mundel, Carl Campbell, and others who've donated generously to the Heindl Fund and the Neuroscience Research Foundation. They've enabled research efforts and contributed to many papers, book chapters, and books over the years.

Robert Goldman, president and co-founder with Ronald Klatz of The American Academy of Anti-Aging Medicine, remains an inspiration regarding physical fitness and balanced living.

To Art and Dan Rooney and the Pittsburgh Steelers organization, I will always be indebted to you for some of the most exciting experiences of my life over the last 30 years. You've always stood by me and have helped to vindicate me from some harsh criticism, and for that I am grateful.

To the McMahon family and Paul Levesque of World Wrestling Entertainment, I deeply appreciate that you've entrusted me with your prized talent. You commit resources, time, and care that few people recognize to improve the health of your athletes.

And to my four daughters—Laura, Lisa, Adara, and Isabella—as well as my dear son, Jonathan, I love you all. I sincerely treasure my memories with you and place great value on the connections we continue to forge. Thanks also go to my sisters, Mary and Lorraine, who've offered unwavering support, love, and encouragement over the years.

NOW TO THOSE PEOPLE who've made this book possible.

Carrie Kennedy, my coauthor, had a marked indefatigability to extract, consider, and then integrate both facts and memories into a seamless and coherent whole, and I appreciate her steadfast dedication to this project. I've gained a new best friend while working with her through this process, and I'm also indebted to her skilled husband, Kevin, for our book's clear and creative design. Margaret Scherbel is largely responsible for *Square One* because she serendipitously introduced me to Carrie several years ago, and she has remained a champion of our book project ever since. Margaret has also helped me finally understand the joy and possibilities of a healthy relationship, and for that, I am humbled and grateful beyond words.

I've relied, as always, on my amazing office staff, particularly my administrative assistant, Karen Hlavac, for keeping me so organized, and senior researcher Dr. Chris Mathyssek for her help with the details. Thanks go to John Tumolo for his friendship as well as his reliable legal counsel, and to John Brabender and his staff at BrabenderCox for their invaluable help in spreading the word about *Square One*. Mark Bolster deserves praise for his outstanding photography work, as does Elizabeth Polen for her proofreading and Megan Kennedy for her fact-checking and organizational assistance.

To Sam Hazo, Rajesh Durbal, and Elizabeth Tyler-Kabara, I cannot thank you enough for sharing your stories so openly and willingly. I value our friendships dearly and know my readers will learn valuable lessons from your inspired approach to living. And to my many colleagues and friends who agreed to read the manuscript and offer comments, corrections, advice, and reviews, I am truly appreciative of your time and support.

And finally, to David Danforth, Dr. William Danforth, Patrick Mulcahy, Anna Kay Vorsteg, and all those involved with the American Youth Foundation: the philosophies of William H. Danforth changed my life. Indeed, they *saved* my life. I've taken the task of putting my story to paper very seriously in the hopes that I can honor the work that you continue to do every day. ☐

CHAPTER ONE: Running on Empty

1   Sonya Lyubomirsky, *The Myths of Happiness: What Should Make You Happy, but Doesn't, What Shouldn't Make You Happy, but Does* (New York: Penguin Press, 2013), 186.

2   Joseph LeDoux, *The Emotional Brain: The Mysterious Underpinnings of Emotional Life* (New York: Simon and Schuster, 1996), 19.

3   Richard Rohr, *Falling Upward: A Spirituality for the Two Halves of Life* (San Francisco: Jossey-Bass, 2011), xx.

4   John S. Uebersax, "Plato's Chariot Allegory," *Works on Psychology* (February 2007), http://www.john-uebersax.com/plato/plato3.htm. Accessed May 2016.

CHAPTER TWO: Out of Balance

1   Rollo May, *Love and Will* (New York: W. W. Norton & Company, Inc., 1969), 243.

2   LeDoux, 40.

3   Dan Ariely, James B. Duke, and William L. Lanier, "Disturbing Trends in Physician Burnout and Satisfaction with Work-Life Balance," *Mayo Clinic Proceedings* 90, no. 12 (2015): 1593–1596, doi:http://dx.doi.org/10.1016/j.mayocp.2015.10.004.

CHAPTER THREE: William Danforth and His Square

1   William H. Danforth, *I Dare You,* 16th ed. (St. Louis: Privately printed, 1954), v.

2   Ibid., 1.

3   Ibid.

4   Ibid., 29.

5   Ibid., 83.

6   Ibid., iii.

7   Ibid., xi.

8   Ibid., 8.

9   Ibid., 51.

10   Ibid., 21.

11   Ibid., 62.

12   Ibid., 22.

CHAPTER FOUR: First Steps

1   All information on this page was taken from triathlonhistory.com. Thanks to Betty Johnstone, wife of the late Jack Johnstone, for her assistance.

CHAPTER FIVE: Body: The Physical Side

1   I never would've guessed that three decades later, I'd be inducted into the National Fitness Hall of Fame, just a few years after Kenneth Cooper had received the same honor. The extensive list of members includes Jack LeLanne, Arnold Schwarzenegger, and Kathy Smith.

2   Masood A. Shammas, "Telomeres, Lifestyle, Cancer, and Aging," *Current Opinions in Clinical Nutrition and Metabolic Care* 14, no. 1 (January 2011): 28–34, doi:0.1097/MCO.0b013e32834121b1.

3   Esther Sternberg, *The Balance Within: The Science Connecting Health and Emotions* (New York: W. H. Freeman, 2000), 5.

4   Henrietta van Praag, Gerd Kempermann, and Fred H. Gage, "Running Increases Cell Proliferation and Neurogenesis in the Adult Mouse Dentate Gyrus," *Nature Neuroscience* 2 (1999): 266–270, doi:10:1038/6368.

     Peter S. Eriksson, Ekaterina Perfilieva, Thomas Björk-Eriksson et al., "Neurogenesis in the Adult Human Hippocampus," *Nature Medicine* 4 (1998): 1313–1317, doi:10.1038/3305.

5   Duke University, "Exercise May Be Just as Effective as Medication for Treating Major Depression," *ScienceDaily*, October 27, 1999, http://www.sciencedaily.com/releases/1999/10/991027071931.htm. Accessed July 2016.

6   E. D. Kantor, C. D. Rehm, J. S. Haas, A. T. Chan, and E. L. Giovannucci, "Trends in Prescription Drug Use among Adults in the United States from 1999–2012," *Journal of the American Medical Association* 314, no. 17 (2015): 1818–1831, doi:10.1001/jama.2015.13766.

     G. M. Cooney, K. Dwan, C. A. Greig, D. A. Lawlor, J. Rimer, F. R. Waugh, M. McMurdo, and G. E. Mead, "Exercise for Depression," *Cochrane Database of Systematic Reviews* 9 (September 2013): CD004366, doi:10.1002/14651858.CD004366.pub6.

7   Duke University Medical Center, "Common Nutrients Fed to Pregnant Mice Altered Their Offspring's Coat Color," *ScienceDaily*, August 1, 2003, http://www.sciencedaily.com/releases/2003/08/030801081754. Accessed July 2016.

8   Daniel H. Pink, *A Whole New Mind: Why Right-Brainers Will Rule the Future* (New York: Riverhead Books, 2006), 238–239.

9   Danforth, 8.

CHAPTER SIX: Soul: The Spiritual Side

1   Danforth, 82.

2   Danforth, 87.

3   Simon Sinek, "How Great Leaders Inspire Action," TEDx *Puget Sound* (September 2009), https://www.ted.com/talks/simon_sinek_how_great_leaders_inspire_action.

4   A. L. Ai, P. Wink, and M. Shearer, "Secular Reverence Predicts Shorter Hospital Length of Stay among Middle-Aged and Older Patients Following Open-Heart Surgery," *Journal of Behavioral Medicine* 34, no. 6 (December 2011): 532–41, doi:10.1007/s10865-011-9334-8.

5   All material about Rajesh Durbal came from personal interviews and email correspondence.

6   Sue McGreevy, "Eight Weeks to a Better Brain," *Harvard Gazette*, January 21, 2011, http://news.harvard.edu/gazette/story/2011/01/eight-weeks-to-a-better-brain/. Accessed May 2016.

7   David Brooks, *The Road to Character* (New York: Random House, 2015), xii.

8   Dan Harris, *10% Happier: How I Tamed the Voice in My Head, Reduced Stress without Losing My Edge, and Found Self-Help That Actually Works: A True Story* (New York: Dey Street Books, 2014), 140.

9   Ibid., 142.

CHAPTER SEVEN: Brain: The Work Side

1   Tait D. Shanafelt, Omar Hasan, Lotte N. Dyrbye, Christine Sinsky, Daniel Satele, Jeff Sloan, and Colin P. West, "Changes in Burnout and Satisfaction with Work-Life Balance in Physicians and the General US Working Population Between 2011 and 2014," *Mayo Clinic Proceedings* 90, no. 12 (December 2015): 1600–1613, doi:http://dx.doi.org/10.1016/j.mayocp.2015.08.023.

2   Mick Oreskovich and James Anderson, "Physician Personalities and Burnout," *Bulletin of the American College of Surgeons*, June 1, 2013, http://bulletin.facs.org/2013/06/personalities-and-burnout/.

3   Louise B. Andrew and Barry E. Brenner, "Physician Suicide," Medscape, July 2, 2016, http://emedicine.medscape.com/article/806779-overview.

4   Valerie Strauss, "Teacher: The Day I Knew for Sure I Was Burned Out," *Washington Post*, December 12, 2014.

5   Ken Robinson, *The Element: How Finding Your Passion Changes Everything* (New York: Penguin Books, 2009), 9.

6   Ibid., 8.

7   All material about Dr. Elizabeth Tyler-Kabara came from personal interviews and email correspondence.

CHAPTER EIGHT: Heart: The Relationship Side

1   Daniel Goleman, *Emotional Intelligence: Why It Can Matter More Than IQ* (New York: Bantam Books, 2006), 33–34.

2   Karen Armstrong, "Metaphysical Mistake: Confusion by Christians between Belief and Reason Has Created Bad Science and Inept Religion," *Guardian*, July 12, 2009.

3   Karen Armstrong, *The Case for God* (New York: Anchor Books, 2010), xiv.

4   Joseph Campbell, *The Power of Myth* (New York: Anchor Books, 1991), 87.

5   Emily Esfahani Smith, "Masters of Love," *Atlantic*, June 12, 2014.

6   All material about Samuel Hazo came from personal interviews and email correspondence.

7   Samuel Hazo, "To All My Mariners in One," *And the time is: Poems*, 1958–2013 (Syracuse, NY: Syracuse University Press, 2014), 82.

8   Goleman, 161.

9   Pink, 174.

10   Mitch Albom, *Tuesdays with Morrie: An Old Man, a Young Man, and Life's Greatest Lesson* (New York: Broadway Books, 1997), 91.

11   Goleman, 36.

12   Gary Chapman, *The 5 Love Languages: The Secret to Love That Lasts* (Chicago: Northfield Publishing, 2010), 15.

13   Ibid.

CHAPTER NINE: Humor, Creativity, and Flow

1   Robinson, 67.

2   Copenhagen Institute of Neurocreativity, "Neurocreativity Mini-Series: An Apple, a Ferrari, and the Human Brain," July 16, 2014, http://neurocreativity.wixsite.com/blog. Accessed January 12, 2016.

3   Gary Wolf, "Steve Jobs: The Next Insanely Great Thing," *Wired*, February 1, 1996.

4   Daniel Goleman, *Social Intelligence: The New Science of Human Relationships* (New York: Bantam Books, 2006), 61.

5   Image adapted from Mihaly Csikszentmihalyi, *Flow: The Psychology of Optimal Experience* (2008; repr., New York: Harper Perennial, 1990), 74.

6   Excerpt from Theodore Roosevelt, "Citizenship in a Republic" (speech, Sorbonne, Paris, France, April 23, 1910).

CHAPTER TEN: The Square Philosophy for Kids

1   Danforth, v.

2   Centers for Disease Control and Prevention, "Childhood Obesity Facts," updated August 17, 2015, https://www.cdc.gov/healthyschools/obesity/facts.htm. Accessed May 2016.

3   Personal interview and email correspondence with Dr. Jamie McNanie.

4   Robert Brooks and Sam Goldstein, *Raising Resilient Children: Fostering Strength, Hope, and Optimism in Your Child* (Lincolnwood, Ill.: Contemporary Books, 2001), 193.

5   Eileen Kennedy-Moore, "What Are Social Skills? Helping Children Become Comfortable and Competent in Social Situations," *Psychology Today*, August 18, 2011.

6   Harper Lee, *To Kill a Mockingbird* (New York: Warner Books, 1960), 30.

7   Danah Boyd, *It's Complicated: The Social Lives of Networked Teens* (New Haven: Yale University Press, 2014), 30.

8   Danforth, 66.

9   Carol Dweck, *Mindset: The New Psychology of Success* (New York: Random House, 2006), 15.

10 Po Bronson, "How Not to Talk to Your Kids: The Inverse Power of Praise," *New York Magazine*, August 3, 2007.

11 Dweck, 48.

12 Robinson, 42.

13 Material in this section came from personal interviews with Anna Kay Vorsteg, campers, and their parents at Camp Merrowvista, Tuftonboro, New Hampshire, in August 2013.

14 Anna Kay Vorsteg, "Preparing the Child for the Path," *American Youth Foundation Blog,* June 22, 2016, https://ayf.com/news-events/blog/preparing-child-path.

15 Danforth, 10.

16 Ibid., 81–82.

CONCLUSION

1   Ibid., 19.

2   Material in this section came from personal interviews conducted while climbing Mt. Kilimanjaro, February 18–24, 2014.

3   Henri Nouwen, *Reaching Out: The Three Movements of the Spiritual Life* (New York: Doubleday, 1986), Foreword.

All photographs were purchased from stock photograpy or available in the public domain with the exceptions of the following:

Cover image of Joe Maroon, Joe Maroon on bike on Table of Contents, and Joe Maroon's prayer necklace (66) by Mark Bolster.

Photo of Joe Maroon in surgery (32) taken by Joseph Unitas of Unitas Photography.

Other personal photos of Joe Maroon (inside front cover, 32, 33, 38, 56) used with his permission.

Portrait of William H. Danforth (37) used with permission by the Danforth family.

Image of Bill Phillips, Don Shanahan, and Jack Johnstone (49) used with permission by Betty Johnstone.

All personal photos of Rajesh Durbal (72, 74, 75) used with his permission.

Personal photo of Elizabeth-Tyler Cabara (92) used with her permission, and photo of Elizabeth with Jan Scheuermann (92) made available through UPMC.

All personal photos of Sam Hazo and his family (105, 107) used with his permission.

Photo of statue of Harmony in Old Economy Village (110) taken by Carrie Kennedy.

Fireplace at Camp Merrowvista (144) taken by Bailey Sheats. Portrait of Anna Kay Vorsteg and AYF campers (147, 148) used with permission by the American Youth Foundation.

Photos from Mount Kilamanjaro (153, 154, 156) used with permission by Joseph Maroon.

Image on spine and next to Pythia Publishing information on back cover is a Greek coin struck in Delphi in 480 BC. Pythia was the name given to the high priestess that acted as the oracle at the Temple of Apollo at Delphi, and the reverse of the coin shows an *omphalos* ("navel") because the Greeks considered Delphi to be the very center of the world. Image by The Classical Numismatic Group, Inc., www.cngcoins.com, CC BY-SA 3.0.